DESIGN DOWN UNDER 2

Contents

DESIGN DOWN UNDER 2

Henry Steiner

Ozmosis by Henry Steiner, Hong Kong
The biggest island or the smallest
continent, Australia has an area similar to
the United States, with the population of
Tokyo, dry flat, sunbaked except at its
edges, this remote land preserved - as
though under a glass dome - plants and
animals which had disappeared from the
rest of the world and men who retain a
complex, sophisticated Stone Age culture
with painting and music precious to
today's artistic awareness.

Just over two centuries ago, this dreaming
giant was invaded by European explorers
and cast-offs, who did their best to re-
create the ambience of Mother England in
alien surroundings, sharing space un
comfortably with the indigenes. After the
Pacific War waves of newcomers from
Central Europe, Italy, Greece, Asia and -
now voluntarily - Britain, added to the
society a fermentation similar to that of
the national beverage, bringing the spices
of Southern Europe and Asia to the
traditionally dull cuisine.

These newly integrated immigrants are
creating what has been optimistically
described as the 'honey-coloured' society,
equidistant to Europe, America and Asia,
with a new and growing sense of
individuality and an interest in language
other than English. But today Australia is
a resentful part of the American cultural
empire, with a lifestyle more closely
resembling California than anywhere in
Britain or Asia.

There is a striking similarity between San
Francisco and Sydney, diametrically
positioned on each edge of the Pacific
Basin. (Having come to this conclusion
myself, I later discovered that Marcello
Minale had made a similar observation in
the first volume of this series.)

Massimo Vignelli *Olaf Leu* *Henry Steiner*

The symptoms of this affinity can be seen
in graphic design. Perhaps the most
obvious representative of the cheerful,
splashy, extroverted manner shared by
many Oz designers - which owes much to
the West Coast 'New Wave' style - is Ken
Done. Amiable, prolific and hugely
successful, Ken happily straddles the
domains of the Matisse and Mammon and
has lectured fellow designers on the
desirability of keeping a share of the
profits generated by their talent. His
oversize prints and sportswear have
already carved a profitable niche in Japan,
and his enterprise spreads acceptance of
Oz design around the world.

Just as there is much design in California
with a more subtle and sensitive feel, so
there are some extremely refined Aussie
designers - like Garry Emery and Brian
Sadgrove.

Homage is due also to Gordon Andrews,
an all-round design pioneer who returned
home from London and Turin to set an
important example for the profession. My
favourite among his projects is the set of
designs for the new dollar banknotes when

final competition will be kept within the home profession; it would be unspeakably silly for Canberra even to consider inviting outsiders.

Now that the spotlight has shifted from Mother England to Uncle Sam, Australian designers should be directing their vitality and marketing flair to the Asia Pacific countries. Ken Cato, for example, is successfully commuting to Tokyo, setting an entrepreneurial example to his colleagues.

After the Mediterranean and the Atlantic, the Pacific is without question the new focus of world attention. It's time more Australian designers explored the backyard beyond the outback.

Olaf Leu

Olaf Leu, Weisbaden

This book, a conscious collection of top designs doubtless constitutes a landmark or a parameter, which, as in the field of sports, advances itself over the years, and overtakes even itself.

Books of this type are documents of the times, important for the present, a focal point for the future. I travelled both these

Australia went metric. Having designed the odd banknote myself, I especially appreciate the way Gordon created a totally Australian identity which goes so much deeper than attractive quotations from aboriginal art.

A limitation which Australian business often imposes on design is the cringe towards so-called expertise from overseas. There have been occasions where specialist services have been successfully imported, but when the '88 Brisbane Expo wanted a mascot emblem, rather than consult, for example, brilliant Melbourne animator/illustrator Alex Stitt (who had already designed a marvellous pavilion within Expo for the Australian Government and who has done some of the brightest postage stamps I've ever seen), the bureaucrats commissioned Walt Disney Studios. Predictably expensive and fatuous, they initially hatched a friendly dingo; given a second try, the Disney artists' best shot was a platypus which closely resembled a blue Donald Duck. The new national flag will be a major project for Australian designers. While several half-baked amateur competitions have already been perpetrated, with generally disastrous outcomes, I trust the

countries - Australia and New Zealand - intensively during winter 1991 for 10 weeks. I can't make anything of the expression "Down under". To me, no continent is above or below. Each country, each continent, to me, is the midpoint, and carries within itself a pulsating heart. Perhaps, or even for sure, those centres, based on which the world was discovered and settled, did exist. Communication during these times was poor. Today, the people of the world are connected more than ever, to a large

extent they are economically dependent on one another. Communication plays an important role in this respect. Communication for commercial services, products and other enterprises, is the function of the factor design. Design renders things conceivable, they are tangible for the eye, the mind, and finally the hand. Many, but not all works, which are presented here, are visually intelligible, comprehensible across the language barrier. As far as this goes, they are good communication items, examples of a "language" which can be understood anywhere in the world. I do not want nor would I like to find the specific Australian or New Zealand "touch". This would restrict the desired comprehensibility and restrict it to those especially initiated. No, this book and its "content" belongs to the world, this spherical, blue planet, of which, please, someone should tell me where to find above and below.

"Down under" may be explainable on the basis of a feeling of lacking, or scarce, economical and cultural centres. For such a large continent, the population density may seem thin to scanty by European standards and the fears of contact amongst European neighbours. In Germany, with its around 80 million inhabitants, one can easily feel like sardines in a can. How free, on the other hand, is the sky and the earth of these islands Australia and New Zealand! Vastness creates greatness - greatness creates freedom. This "feeling of vastness" may in future play a more important role in the Australian design, as

far as one can dissociate oneself from the "Down under feeling", an expression which is used by other people to refer to Australia. Communication and its branches can alter this social "Down under feeling", withdraw its existence. During my long trip, I went to many cities, talked to many colleagues, and saw their works. This was the case for Perth, Adelaide, Melbourne, Canberra, Sydney, Brisbane, Auckland and Wellington. I do not give preference to any city over the others. I have no understanding of the skirmish between Melbourne and Sydney even though the same can be found in my country. Everywhere I have seen things which were natural to me, visually and verbally well-founded and presentable. The students were neither better nor worse, nor different, they could just as well have been German students. Again, I do not like to find differences. So, where then is the specifically Australian or New Zealand character? It is the people, originally from all quarters of the globe, who live in this vastness, and who are just starting to comprehend the feeling of this largeness. Some of this "comprehending", that is to say, self identity is portrayed in this book.

Massimo Vignelli

Massimo Vignelli, New York
In the spring of 1991, I gave a talk in Melbourne and met hundreds of students of graphic design coming from all sides of Australia. Their interest, talent and enthusiasm represents one of the best investments of that country's future. Their generation of teachers is committed to quality and dedicated to making a better environment for everyone. Graphic design in Australia has definitely come of age.

One of the most exciting feelings in Australia is the sense of energy in the air. People want to make things better; there is a general thrust toward quality. Restaurants are beautiful, food is excellent (an important and very revealing sign) and wine has incredibly beautiful labels. There is a great quantity of beautiful buildings and public structures; shops and products reveal a fresh level of taste of a society in a wholesome state of growth. Graphic design, product design, and packaging design are all very much involved in this process. There seems to be awareness of the integrity of design in the production process. There seems to be awareness of history, a pride of the past, a sense of continuity.

Australian graphic design is the product of a culture that thinks in global terms, a culture spanning beyond its physical boundaries reaching globally for improvements and refinements while asserting its own integrity and expression. The outstanding, highly civilized design

approaches to signage in public places (such as the new Parliament in Canberra or the Powerhouse Museum in Sydney) are just a few of the many excellent examples one encounters throughout Australia. The magnificent, elegant work of Garry Emery, the forceful work of Ken Cato, and the witty, refined labels of Barry Tucker are just a few of the examples of a culture that has found its own way to express its values.

I am extremely impressed by the high level of professionalism of Australian graphic designers. The multiple offices of Cato, the extremely beautiful office of Garry Emery and the many others as well, are evidence of a profession that has not only come of age, but is asserting its values, its reason of being, and its role in the society. I will also say that our Australian colleagues, perhaps more than any others that I know, have advanced our profession by refining its role and projecting it into the business world. At the technical level, the state of the art of Australian graphic design is high, advanced and sophisticated; it is ready to face the enormous changes brought to our profession by all new technologies. Australian design has a strong vernacular tradition with a folksy undercurrent that enriches the expressions of contemporary design, as many products, labels and packages attest. A terrific book by Mimmo Cozzolino reveals the strength of popular graphics through the ages of this young country. The influence of well structured design is evident in many of the publications and brochures one sees as well as the influence of design trends from all over the world. This is a sign of vitality, a response to the global culture in which we live. Australian designers are showing us not only the outstanding quality of their designs but also that good design can be good business without capitulating to the pressures of marketing, shallowness or greed.

From down under to all the way up!

Elda Charous

Annette Harcus

Neil Turner

Ken Cato

John Nowland

Raymond Bennett

Mark Adams

Mimmo Cozzolino

Ned Culic

Elda Charous

Elda Charous was born in the latter part of this century near the clutter of signage that was then Sydney's bohemian King's Cross. Bedazzled by the colour and typography, she survived a disciplined childhood and measured adolescence at the hands of nuns and busy Italian parents. A handful of remarkable designer/tutors helped her towards her graduation at 'Old Randwick' in 1974. After a brief stint as a sales lady, Elda began working with Australia's very own design doyen, Gordon Andrews. She counts his friendship and influence as formative in bringing tasteful notions of texture to her work. She acknowledges the part that each design collaboration has had in shaping her own appreciation of the elements that combine to create stimulating and successful design.

Still bedazzled by colour and typography, Elda's work and that of her Sydney studio, Kameruka Design Group, bring colour and sensitivity to the corporate publications of big tough companies, interest and strength to the small. Her work is always present at a celebration of the best in Australian Graphic Design.

Annette Harcus

Annette Harcus was born in Sydney in 1959 and graduated from Sydney College of the Arts (now University of Technology) in 1980, with a Bachelor of Arts in Visual Communication.
In 1982, Annette founded Annette Harcus Design and since then has focused on corporate identity programs and communication, architectural and environmental signage and packaging. Annette has undertaken numerous design projects for some of Australia's most recognised and prestigious companies and organisations. She is also currently engaged in a variety of design projects in other countries including Singapore, Fiji, Hong Kong, Indonesia, France, and India. In under ten years, Annette has established herself as one of Australia's most outstanding designers. Her work has been featured in many international publications and has won numerous awards.

Judges

DESIGN DOWN UNDER 2

John Nowland

John Nowland was born in Melbourne in 1949. In 1971 he completed his studies at the Royal Melbourne Institute of Technology. He then worked for Brian Sadgrove & Associates followed by Emery, Fowler-Brown Design. There he opened his own design office in 1974. His work has received numerous industry awards.

Mimmo Cozzolino

Mimmo Cozzolino was born in Italy in 1949 and came to Australia in 1961. In 1986 he formed his fourth studio, Cozzolino/Ellett Design D'Vision, when he joined designer/illustrator Philip Ellett.

In 1987 he co-founded the Australian Graphic Design Association which now has over 500 members across Australia. Mimmo's enduring interest is Australian trademarks. He's working on a follow-up volume to Symbols of Australia which he first published in 1980. He feels that with Australians' growing interest in exploring their own culture, there are exciting possibilities for more designers to document and publish other areas of Australian graphic design history. "For instance, when are we going to see a definitive visual history of Australian packaging?" he asks.

Mimmo is a frequent participant on national and state judging panels for design and advertising awards.

Neil Turner

Neil Turner completed a degree in graphic design at Curtin University in Perth, Western Australia.

Shortly after, in 1978 he established Turner Design which has grown into a multi-disciplinary graphic design consultancy involved in the areas of corporate identity, brand identity, packaging, signage and communication design. Neil has been involved in many of the major graphic design projects in Perth in recent years and that work has been recognised and awarded both locally and nationally.

Raymond Bennett

Raymond Bennett is design director of Raymond Bennett Design. Initially active in the field of industrial design, he later concentrated his work in the areas of packaging, corporate identity programs, annual report design and corporate financial communications.

His company has undertaken projects both locally and internationally, and has handled work for some of Australia's largest companies through to smaller organisations.

Raymond Bennett's established reputation and standard of work excellence has been acknowledged through numerous major awards, including the Prince Phillip Award for Australian Design; the National Print Awards; the Packaging Council of Australia; and prizes in other industry competitions in Australia and overseas.

His work has been published in: -
View from Australia
World Graphic Design Now
Noah (The directory of International package design)
World Trademarks & Logotypes II
Last year he was one of the speakers at "Envision 16", an annual design conference held in California U.S.A.

Mark Adams

Mark Adams was born in Kentucky, USA in 1953, but grew up in New Zealand. He began his career in advertising, working as an art director for several years before studying graphic design at the University of Canterbury School of Fine Arts. He also trained as a teacher and taught graphic design. Like many Kiwis, he has also worked abroad, in advertising and design in the USA and London.

Returning to Auckland he joined one of New Zealand's first multi-discipline design groups, Designforces, before establishing his own company Design Matrix. In 1989, Design Matrix joined with Debeer Designs to form Debeer Adams Associates.

Debeer Adams is one of New Zealand's most highly regarded design groups, with a reputation for creativity and innovation. The principals, Mark and partner Peter Debeer, are also the group's principal designers. Their work for many of New Zealand's major companies and organisations has been published internationally - and gained them a collection of design awards unequalled in the country.

Mark is a Fellow of the New Zealand Society of Designers, and as President from 1988, was heavily involved in the Society's revitalisation. During this period, a full-time secretariat was established, 'The Best Graphic Design Awards' were introduced, and the Society grew from less than sixty to over six hundred members. As one of its principal proponents, he has also been integrally involved in the formation of the Designers Institute of New Zealand.

Ned Culic

Ned Culic is a versatile designer/ illustrator with considerable experience in all areas of graphic communication. His work has been featured in international design annuals and many local publications including Design Down Under Number One.

Ned has served on judging panels for industry associations and has been involved in design education throughout Australia.

He works on a diverse range of projects for advertising, publishing and direct clients. Much of his work has an illustrative bias.

Ken Cato

Ken Cato is Chairman of Cato Design Inc Pty Ltd, a company which was founded 21 years ago. Cato Design is the largest design studio in the southern hemisphere, with a Head Office in Melbourne and offices in Sydney, Perth, Auckland, Tokyo, Singapore, Hong Kong, Indonesia, Kuala Lumpur and New York. As a graphic designer, Ken's work has earned him an international reputation and his designs have been published in every major graphic arts magazine throughout the world. He has won numerous Australian and international design awards for projects as diverse as the 1996 Melbourne Olympic Candidature, to Australian Airlines' corporate identity. A frequent speaker at art colleges and professional seminars in Australia and overseas, he has also compiled major design publications and reference works, including "The View From Australia", "Design for Business" and "First Choice".

Communication Graphics

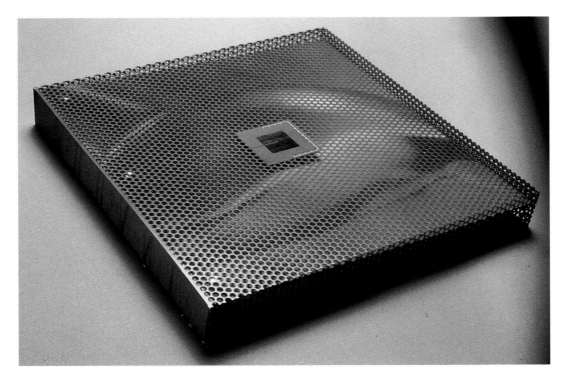

Urbane Studio Promotional Portfolio

Designer Jeff Thornton · Cato Design Inc

Client Urbane Publicity Inc

Opposite Page

Kite Day Promotional Material

Designers Anna Cauchi, Anthony Ginns

Ginns Design Group Pty Ltd

Art Director Anthony Ginns

Illustrator Ginns Design Group Pty Ltd

Typographer Anna Cauchi

Client Australian Graphic

Design Association

Sales Kit for Business Systems

Software Manufacturers

Designer David Roffey

David Roffey Design

Illustrator Mark Tremlett

Client Micropay

Edge Magazine

Designer Ken Cato · Cato Design Inc

Client Cato Design Inc

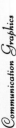

rich

ROBERT WILK

THE NEW RICH IN JAPAN

ANDY & US

BEFORE

UPDATED

For example, corrugated
cardboard is a material
limited to industrial
packaging, with
a reputation for
utilitarianism rather
than shelf appeal. It

Opposite Page

Self Promotion 'Peace On Earth'

Designer Paul Nolan · Nolan Design

Programme Guide **Designer** Cato Design Inc

Client Melbourne International Festival Committee

Melbourne Olympic Bid Books

Designer Ken Cato · Cato Design Inc

Client The Melbourne Olympic

Candidature 1996

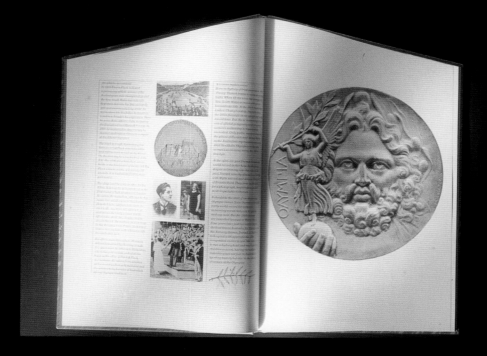

'EOS' Brochure **Designer** Emery Vincent Associates

Art Director Garry Emery **Client** Spire Properties

Opposite Page

Go Karting Invitation

Designer Michael Marzi · Marzi Design

Client KLP Marketing Team

ROBIN DYKE ARAIA
DIRECTOR

Robin Dyke worked with Harry Seidler & Associates before receiving the Royal Australian Institute of Architects Silver Medal as the top architectural graduate in Australia. In 1978 he established his own practice, and received an RAIA Merit Award in 1981 for the Hampden Court Apartment building. He joined Daryl Jackson as Senior Architect in 1982, and became a partner in 1985.

Robin Dyke is acknowledged as a talented and thoughtful architect. Under his direction the practice has attracted a group of experienced professionals who value and support his commitment to good design.

This commitment begins with a thorough practical analysis of the possibilities of the site and the client's needs. Ideas are tested, and opportunities in composition and construction are explored. Robin combines the ability to conceive of space in three dimensions with the skill of clearly conveying his ideas on paper. His management of the design developments and documentation process is grounded in a first hand appreciation of the craft and science of building.

RAIA Councillor, 1992. Juror RAIA Chapter Awards 1979, 1989. Course Advisory Committee, University of Technology, Sydney 1988, 1989.

Education
B. Arch (Hons 1), NSW Institute of Technology, 1975.

Registration
Chartered Architect, NSW.

Professional Membership
Associate, Royal Australian Institute of Architects.

Trellini is a showcase for a men's suit fashion label. In a rectangular tenancy, its space defines a curved wall that flanks an arc. The over-hip is length and strong. The interior is a materialist set and the emphasis is on colour. Glass windows to the store like theatrical floats. A concrete slab is now the landmark and the sun-shy stepped construction is expressive and industrial.

Daryl Jackson
Brian Dice
Greg D'Amico
Phil Moore

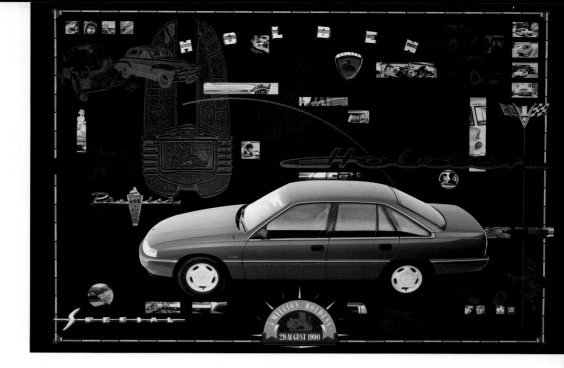

GMH 5 Millionth Holden Poster Designer Philip Ellett
Cozzolino/Ellett Design D'Vision Art Director Mimmo
Cozzolino Finished Artist Carmel Raccosta Typographer
Philip Ellett Client General Motors Holden

Opposite Page

Profile for Architects

Designer Anne Foster

Ross Barr & Associates Pty Ltd

Photographer Gerrit Fokkema

Art Director Ross Barr

Illustrator Daryl Jackson

Robin Dyke Pty Limited

Typographer Anne Foster

Client Daryl Jackson

Robin Dyke Pty Limited

Melbourne Docklands

Designer Chris Perks · Cato Design Inc

Client The Committee for Melbourne

Annual

REPORT

AUSTRALIAN FILM COMMISSION

1990.

Radio Australia Stamp & Envelope

Designer Brian Sadgrove

Brian Sadgrove & Associates

Client Australia Post

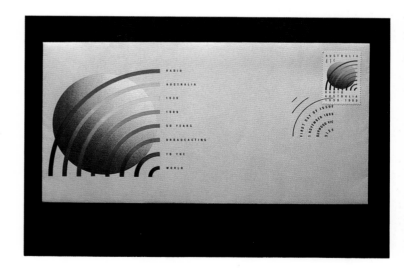

Opposite Page

1990 Annual Report

Designer Isabel Gaven Design Pty Limited

Illustrator Michael Golding

Typographer Isabel Gaven Design

Pty Limited

Client Australian Film Commission

Property Development Brochure

Designer Emery Vincent Associates

Art Director Garry Emery

Client Bridge End Development

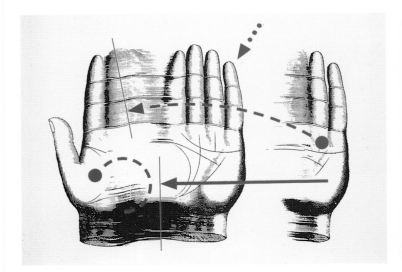

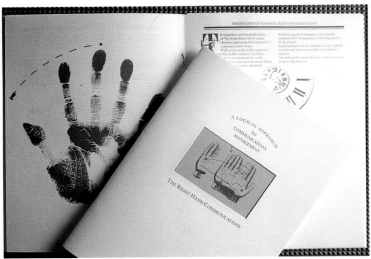

Self-Promotion Brochure

Designer Ken Cato · Cato Design Inc

Client The Right Hand Communications

Pty Limited

Sports Calendar **Designers** Michelle Ryan, Adam Fowler, Brett
Gullan, David Blyth, Anna Cunningham, Michael Bartzis, John
Sellitto, John Pezos, Michelle Ryan, Dominique Falla,
Simon O'Halloran, Michelle MacDonald, Mathew Windebank
Photographer Ray Kinnane **Art Directors** John Bassani,
Keith McEwan · Swinburne School of Design YR3 Design Group
Client Hawthorn Football Club

Type Designer Emery Vincent Associates

Art Director Garry Emery **Client** Artspec Typefounders

GASAA
**For pre-press houses
it's everything
from a watchdog to a
war cry**

The Graphic Arts Services Association of Australia is the only officially recognised association dedicated to serving the interests of pre-press houses in Australia. The Association was first registered under the Commonwealth Arbitration Act in 1933 and membership now comprises companies engaged in Typesetting, design and artwork, Photoengraving, Photolithography (film preparation and platemaking), Photogravure cylinder making, Photopolymer plates/cylinders and rubber stereos, and Screenprinting preparation. Additionally, organisations undertaking in-house platemaking principally for their own use may be admitted as Associate members. Through its national secretariat, GASAA represents members with a unified voice on a range of pertinent issues. The Association liaises with Government departments and trade unions, represents the industry at Commissions, reviews technical and trading matters with suppliers and practices a representative viewpoint in industrial disputes. GASAA fosters understanding and knowledge within the pre-press industry by staging the major industry event, the Annual National Convention, which includes well-attended technical and business seminars. Throughout the year, opportunities are created for members to have regular meetings and discussions with their national and international colleagues, competitors and representatives of associated organisations. Day to day, the secretariat is available to members for assistance and advice regarding industrial issues, government regulations, interpretation of awards, taxation matters, terms of trading and technical developments. In an ever-changing industry, faced with increasing commercial and government demands and complex issues associated with advanced technologies, GASAA safeguards the interests of pre-press houses, provides a forum for dialogue, and assists its members to improve their productivity and profitability.

**Today the pre-press
industry offers its
apprentices and trainees
a superior image,
outstanding memory
and fourth generation
language**

Pre-press is an industry with great traditions, but its progress has never been hampered by these traditions. These days, computers contribute to every aspect of the pre-press phase of print production. Indeed, on first impressions, a pre-press house could easily be mistaken for a computer bureau. The clean, quiet, push-button environment is a far cry from the early process engraving operations in which journeymen and apprentices engaged in their exacting craft amidst pungent odours, wet collodion coating, sticky 'dragon's blood' resin and messy fish glue. An apprentice or trainee entering the industry today is provided with varied and intensive training and an exceptional career opportunity. The prerequisites are a flair for colour balance, an appreciation of aesthetics, and a devotion to detail. As well, the good communicator will play an increasingly important role in the industry as clients become more interested and involved in the pre-press process. The capabilities of computers, with their considerable memory capacity, enhanced image resolution and, now, artificial intelligence software, are providing new potentials and challenges. As technology expands the horizons of pre-press processes, young people have a unique opportunity to contribute to the development and application of innovative techniques. If you're interested in learning more about a career in the pre-press industry, contact GASAA for information and assistance.

Stage 1
Initiation
Concept
Design and
Layout
Text
Photography or
Illustration

**The Print
Production
Cycle**

**Stage 2
Pre-press
Typesetting
Finished art
Manual or
Electronic
Pagination
Separations
Conventional or
Computer
Imaging
Proofing
Machine or
Chemical
Platemaking
Offset Plates
Engravings
Flexographic or
Polymer Plates
and Gravure
Cylinders
Delivery
to printer
Conventional
Facsimile Cable
or Satellite**

**The start
and finish
are of no
value if the
steps in the
middle
aren't
perfect**

Stage 3
Printing
Paper
Printing
Distribution

**Which
companies
are
essential
in the print
production
process
but never
hit the
headlines?**

2

S L U M B E R

PAGE 14

AT THE HIGH TIDE MARK OF INNOVATION,

THERE IS A NEW WAVE OF NEW ZEALAND

DESIGNERS WHOSE WORK IS

FRESH, INSPIRED AND REFRESHING.

HUMPHREY IRIN AND HIS SERVING TABLE

PHOTOGRAPHED BY NARU SAMESHIMA.

PHOTOGRAPHY BILLEN BETTWEISER
TEXT PEERA DILLAR

HAURAK I NORTH WEST WIND

A RANDOM COLLECTION OF
COTTAGES AND BACHES POPULATE WAIHEKE
ISLAND, A HAVEN FOR HOLIDAYMAKERS AND ARTISTS
OFF THE SHELTERED EAST COAST
OF AUCKLAND.
QUIETLY INVERTED AMID THE SLEEPY
SCENE IS THE UNASSUMING
HOUSE AND STUDIO OF THE POTTER
CHRISTINE THACKER.

5

Matthew's doorhandles, Toby's lights,
Humphrey's tables. The same
names keep popping up in all the
INNOVATIVE Auckland interiors. They make up a
close-knit, keen group of DESIGNERS
very conscious of nature and
their surroundings.

5 AUCKLAND DESIGNERS

Photography NARU SAMESHIMA
Art Direction Alyson Bell
Text JONATHAN TURNER

The furniture, fountains and fittings designed by MATTHEW VON STURMER suggest the forms of
prehistoric animals with a touch of space-age technology. "I go fishing and surfing, I'm very aware of
living on an island. My designs are often oriented to marine life, to the ocean, to the harbour." Originally
a jeweller, Matthew is a strong believer in the hands-on approach to design, an enthusiastic witness
of the change from the initial sketch to the final polish. His most recent works in wood and metals
illustrate a new diversity, appropriating industrial materials and elements bought from shops that sell
agricultural machinery. The minimal yet sophisticated tables and chairs designed by HUMPHREY IRIN
accentuate their own methods of assembly. The wooden components are bolted together or meet in a
simple joint. "My designs explain their own construction. No trickery." Sidetracked from a degree in
economics, Irin believes in the idea of furniture as cultural objects. "They can carry meaning in the
same way as a painting or a piece of sculpture." MARILYN SAINTY goes for the good finish. Her
chests-of-drawers, bar stools, and desks, mostly made from satiny wooden veneers, combine the spartan
with the feminine. The rollicking curves and gentle forms of her furniture recall the flowing lines of
the clothes she also designs. "I start off by folding bits of paper," she says of her spontaneous design
method. "Sometimes I just measure in the air with a tape-measure. Then someone transfers all the info
onto a computer screen." From tables to lamps, from garden chairs to jewellery, the designs of STEPHANE
RONDEL retain a certain huggable quality. They are affectionate not bombastic. Trained as a
mechanical engineer, Stephane is also an expert on inflatable architecture. "My style is Nouveau Baroque.
It's warm, not bulky." The son of a well-known sculptor, TOBY TWISS built himself his first forge at
the age of 14. Since then, he's made beds, tables, lamps and a few big sofas from steel. Currently, he
is working on bronze, floral showerheads. "I love the idea of the Industrial Revolution and Victoriana,
when they managed to make very decorative objects using industrial techniques." The studio he set
up recently with Matthew Von Sturmer is a good symbol of the creative energy of design in Auckland
today – where the young designers bypass formal training and invent truly original furniture. •

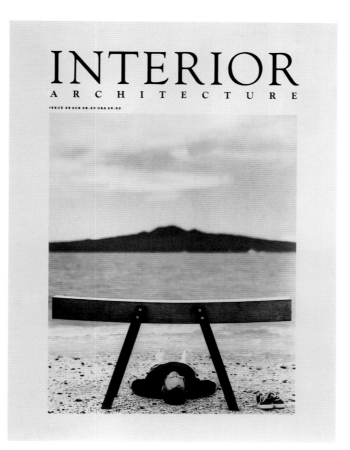

Magazine Article

Typographers Alyson Bell,

Donna Cavanough **Designers** Alyson Bell,

Donna Cavanough, Michelle Pullen

Art Director Alyson Bell

Design Group YPMA Publications

Client Interior Architecture

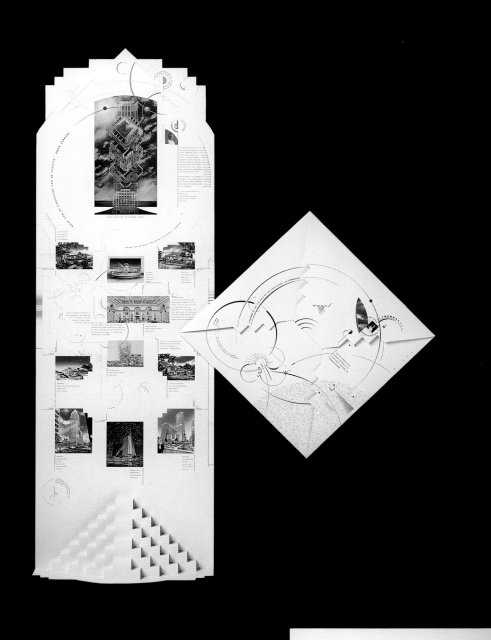

Opposite Page

Promotional Piece Designers Dennis Veal, Kel Naughton,

Paul Nolan · Dennis Veal Design **Art Directors** Kel Naughton,

Dennis Veal **Illustrator** Jane Grealy **Typographers** Kel Naughton,

Paul Nolan **Client** Jane Grealy

Direct Mail Promotion Designers Tim Lyddon, Anna Cauchi

Ginns Design Group Pty Ltd **Photographer** Brad Harris

Art Director Anthony Ginns **Typographer** Anna Cauchi

Client Brad Harris Photography

Opposite Page

Graph Poster Designer Brian Sadgrove

Brian Sadgrove & Associates

Client Rothschild Bank

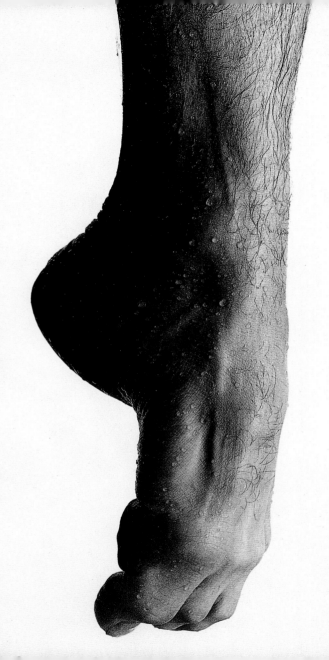

Sydney

Dance

Company

Annual

Report

1988

SYDNEY DANCE

Corporate Brochure for Security/Commercial Printer

Designer Gregory Bridges · Inhaus Design Pty Ltd

Photographer Paul Austin **Client** John Sands Pty Ltd

Opposite Page/Below

Dance Company Annual Report

Designer Phil Ritchie

Ritchie Thornburn Design

Photographer Mark Ritchie

Client Sydney Dance Company

GOLD AWARD

SILVER AWARD

BRONZE AWARD

BEST OF YEAR AWARD

CONTENTS

XIV Beautiful Beetles on Byronic

Designer David Lancashire

David Lancashire Design

Illustrators Various

Typography Godfrey Fawcètt

Client Dalton Fine Paper

Opposite Page/Left

Award Annual 1990

Designers Eugene Rea, James Mortimer

Roberts, Shane Gibson · Bluetree Pty Ltd

Photographer Graham Monro

Art Director Eugene Rea

Illustrators Every Picture Tells A Story

Typographer Shane Gibson

Client Award Annual

Brochure for Country Retreat

Designer Tanja Brjoc

Tanja Brjoc Design

Photographer Richard Millott

Typographer Delmont Typographer

Pty Ltd **Client** Stonelea

Opposite Page

Gellibrand Estate Williamstown

Brochure Designer Alan Marshall

Marshall Arts Graphic Design

Illustrator Ned Culic

Client Torcassio Developments

Corporate Profile

Designer Martine Zajacek

Media Five Australia Pty Ltd

Photographer Richard Stringer

Art Director Sue Ogilvie

Client Media Five Australia

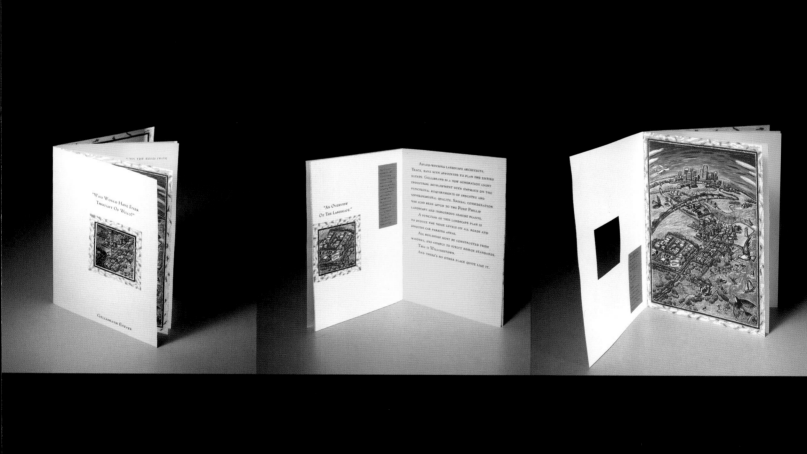

Sportstar Poster

Designers Dennis Veal, Paul Nolan

Dennis Veal Design

Illustrator Paul Nolan

Typographer Dennis Veal

Client Heritage Building Society

Christmas Card Designer Jane Merrick

Swinburne School of Design

Art Director Toni Street

Client Swinburne School of Design

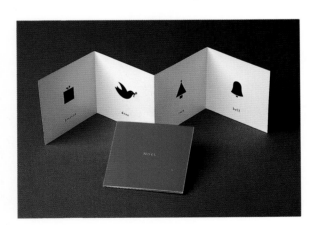

Brochure **Designer** Jeff Thornton

Cato Design Inc

Client Telecom Technologies Pty Ltd

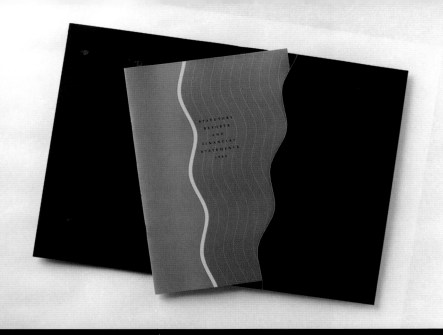

We at CHASE AMP BANK

are committed to being

among the leaders in

providing banking

services in Australia.

This vision of excellence

is realised through our

people, our industry

expertise, our innovation

and our delivery of

quality services.

Opposite Page

Annual Report for Insurance Co

Designers Dagmar Ackerman,

Paula Chrystello · TCG Graphic Design

Photographer John Love

Art Director Dagmar Ackerman

Typographer Paula Chrystello

Client Chase AMP

Menus and Appetitos

Designer Kevin Wilkins · Siren

Client Arnolds Systems Australia

Zoo Carousel Designer Sue Mawer

Desmond Freeman Associates **Illustrator** Dunka Pradzinski

Client Perth Zoo

Opposite Page/Above

Countrylink Holiday Brochure Designer Tim Lyddon

Ginns Design Group Pty Ltd **Photographer** Various

Art Director Anthony Ginns **Typographer** Tim Lyddon

Client Countrylink

EVA REVIEW

Writing on Walls

February 1994

Issue Number One

Melbourne office:
80 Market Street South Melbourne
Victoria 3205 Australia
Telephone (03) 699 3833 Facsimile (3) 690 7373

Sydney office:
Level Four 357 Sussex Street Sydney
New South Wales 2222 Australia
Telephone (2) 267 8844 Facsimile (2) 267 8833

ABC

1

BOVIS VINCENT ASSOCIATES

Poster for Paper Manufacturers

Designer Philip Ellett

Cozzolino/Ellett Design D'Vision

Art Director Mimmi Cozzolino

Illustrator Philip Ellett

Typographer Philip Ellett

Client Tomasetti Paper

Opposite Page

'EVA' Self Promotion Brochure

Designer Emery Vincent Associates

Art Director Garry Emery

Client Emery Vincent Associates

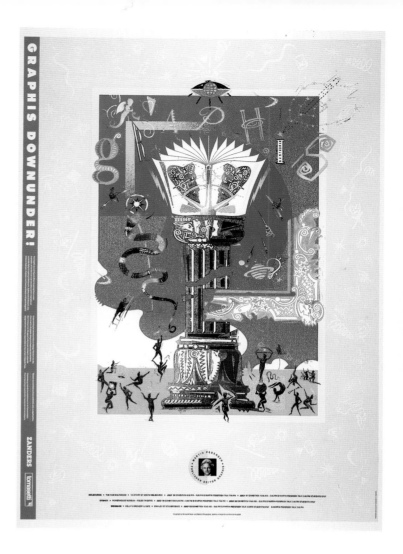

Publication 'First Choice'

Designer Ken Cato · Cato Design Inc

Client Graphic-Sha

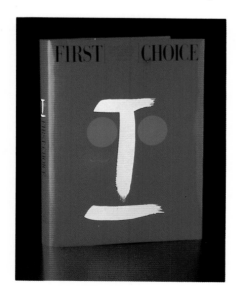

NOMINATING WISDOM...

Such is our vision for the Australia Prize. We
seek your assistance in fulfilling our purpose
by asking for the nomination of a person or group.

of up to four fellows, for your professional
organisation, to have made an outstanding contribution to
the Australian Prize is awarded to all regardless

IF YOU DO
NOT RAISE
YOUR EYES
YOU WILL
THINK
YOU'RE AT
THE
HIGHEST
POINT.

— Antonio Porchia

Opposite Page

Information Brochure

Designer FHA Design

Photographer David Perryman

Client Dept of Industry
Technology & Commerce

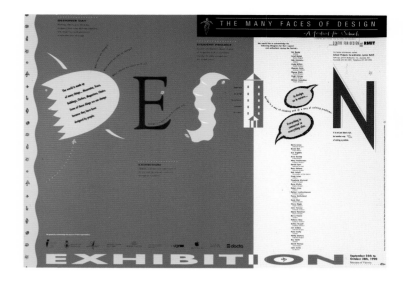

'The Many Faces of Design Festival'

Exhibition Poster

Designer Shane Nagle
Cocoon Design Consultancy

Client RMIT Centre for Design

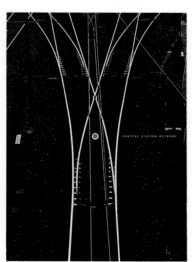

Network Brochure

Designers Russell Springham,
Jeffrey Stewart

Photographer Simon Cowling

Art Director Russell Springham

Client Central Station

DEUS EX MACHINA
1989

Exhibition Catalogue

Designer Michael Trudgeon

Crowd Productions Pty Limited

Photographer Dominic Lowe

Art Director Michael Trudgeon

Typographer Michael Trudgeon

Client Deus Ex Machina Inc

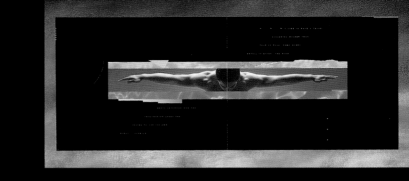

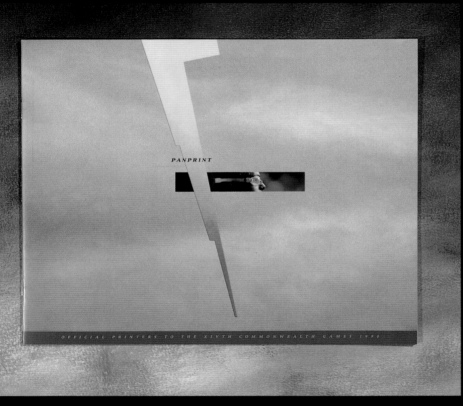

PANPRINT

OFFICIAL PRINTERS TO THE XIVTH COMMONWEALTH GAMES 1990

Opposite Page

Profile for Printing Company

Designers Margaret McGrath, Kel Marsh

Kel Marsh Graphic Design Ltd

Photographer Kim Christensen **Art Director** Kel Marsh

Typographer Margaret McGrath **Client** Panprint

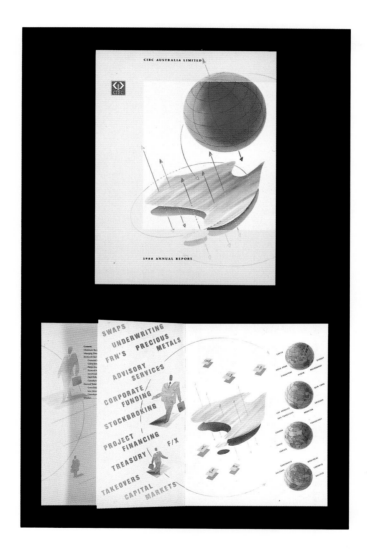

Annual Report for a Merchant Bank

Designer Andrew Gadsby · Gallaher & Associates

Photographer Rowan Fotheringham **Illustrator** Patrice Guilbert

Client CIBC Australia Limited

Opposite Page

**Women in Sport
and Physical
Activity Booklet
Designer** Isabel
Gaven Design
Pty Limited
Illustrator
Sue Ninham
Typographer
Isabel Gaven Design
Pty Limited
Client NSW
Department of
Sport, Recreation
and Racing

Publication 'Melbourne By Melbourne'

Designer Ken Cato · Cato Design Inc **Client** The Melbourne

Olympic Candidature 1996

Communication Graphics

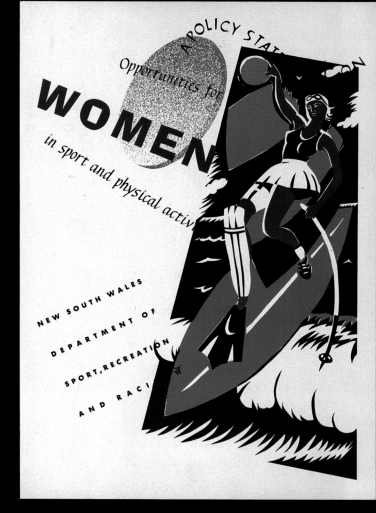

A POLICY STATEMENT

Opportunities for

WOMEN

in sport and physical activity

NEW SOUTH WALES
DEPARTMENT OF
SPORT, RECREATION
AND RACING

OBJECTIVE 5

That the community recognise and accept the importance of women having access to sport and physical activity opportunities.

Strategy

The use of role models to emphasise the benefits of a healthy lifestyle of sport and physical activity.

The use of commercial sponsorship to enhance the quality of the services provided is a longstanding departmental policy. It will be further expanded by seeking sponsorship and co-operation from outside agencies in situations where it is practicable to place emphasis upon the benefits of quality sport and physical activity opportunities for women.

Secondly, the media will be encouraged to ensure that the amount, style and presentation of coverage given to women in sport is fair, and of improved quality.

Thirdly, the use of role models will be actively promoted. Women who possess special talents in the areas of sport and physical activity will be identified so that suitable steps can be taken to enhance their public profile.

Strategy

To stress to executives within commerce and industry the benefits of employing staff who are fit, active and who regularly participate in sport and physical activity.

Industry and commerce need to be convinced of the cost effectiveness of establishing a fitness programme which their employees can access easily. This can be done statistically and by providing examples of successful programmes which allow employees to incorporate fitness into their weekly routine, with the enhancement of both commitment and productivity.

This is yet another area where sponsorship will be sought, this time in promoting the benefits which flow from quality sport and physical activity opportunities for women, whether they be employed in the public sector or in private enterprise.

(15)

OBJECTIVE 6

That women are motivated to participate in sport and physical activity.

Strategy

To highlight women with special ability and to focus on their development so that as role models they may be used to encourage women to participate in sport and recreation opportunities.

As proposed under Objective Five, namely to facilitate media coverage of women engaged in sport and physical activity, and enhancing the public profile of women with special talents, will also serve the dual function of encouraging women to become involved in these activities themselves.

Strategy

To direct the attention of sporting, organisations, schools, community groups, parents and children to the benefits of quality, regular, ongoing, participation in sport and physical activity by women.

Attitudes developed through participation in junior sports often help to determine lifelong sporting philosophies. Through the perceived benefits to be gained, the Department plans to encourage the Department of Education, as well as sporting organisations, to support junior sport, particularly at the level of mixed participation and modified sports at primary school level and at club level.

In a separate course of action, a specific sport will be identified as a pilot project and resources directed to assist in the marketing of it. From the experience gained, a package will be developed for wider distribution to other sports.

Strategy

To concentrate on supporting and encouraging women to become more involved at all levels of sports administration, coaching, and participation in New South Wales.

Leadership development to be promoted by encouraging the participation of women in Sports Development Programmes.

The Department is always concerned to ensure that State sporting associations have the backing of an effective administrative and coaching structure. To circumvent any bias towards the employment of only male staff, sporting organisations are to be reminded of the provisions of the Anti-Discrimination Act, particularly in respect of the application of Equal Employment Opportunity principles in the employment of staff.

Positive discrimination towards the enrolment of women in sports development courses has a trial period is envisaged through organisational and promotional processes.

In the Department's own funding decisions, steps will be taken to ensure that available finance is distributed equitably between males and females. In appropriate circumstances, other funding bodies will be encouraged to adopt and maintain a similar equitable funding policy.

(17)

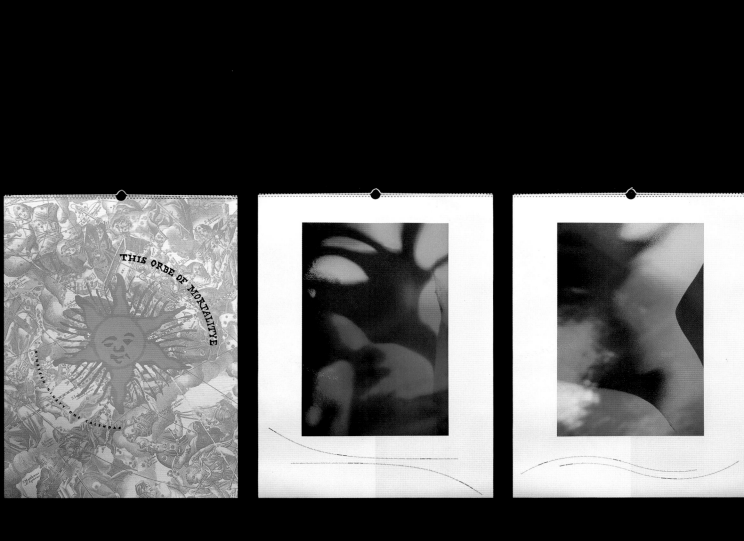

Architect Magazine April/May issue

Designer Emery Vincent Associates

Art Director Garry Emery

Client Royal Australian Institute

of Architects

Opposite Page

1991 Self Promotion Calendar

Designer Tony Di Donato

Asprey Di Donato Design

Photographer James Cant

Art Director Peter Asprey

Typographer Peter Asprey

Profile for Building Company Designers Sara Beesley,

Vanessa Rowe · Linear Design Studio **Photographer** Roel Loopers

Illustrator Cherry Barlowe **Typographer** Sara Beesley

Client Doubikin Constructions Pty Limited

Opposite Page

Sales Brochure for Extensive Property

Development Designer FHA Design

Photographer James Cant, various

Client The Como Project

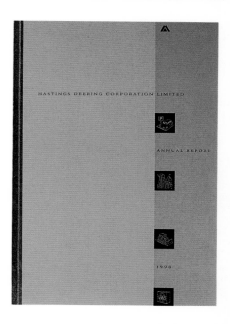

1989 & 1990 Annual Reports

for Diverse Industrial Company

Designer David Roffey

David Roffey Design

Illustrator Mark Tremlett

Client Hastings Deering

Corporation Limited

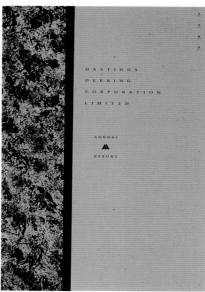

Leeuwin Estate Concert 1990

Designer Paul Dennis · Turner Design

Art Director Neil Turner

Illustrator Paul Dennis

Typographer Paul Dennis

Client Leeuwin Estate

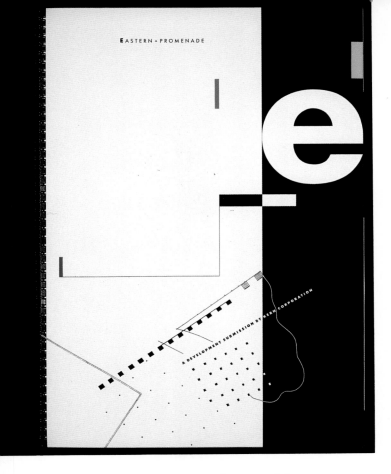

EASTERN · PROMENADE

A DEVELOPMENT SUBMISSION BY KERN CORPORATION

Poster 'Design-A-Kite-Day'

Designers Nelson Leong, Stephen

Harrington, Kuen Kam · Nelson Leong

Art Direction & Design

Art Director Nelson Leong

Illustrator Nelson Leong

Typographers Kuen Kam, Stephen

Harrington **Client** Australian Graphic

Design Association

'Eastern Promenade'

Designer Emery Vincent Associates

Art Director Garry Emery

Client Kern Corporation

Enterprise Workshop Certificates

& Folder Designers Andrew Boddy/

Sue Mawer · Marblist Pegi Deangelis

Client West Australian Enterprise

Workshop

Opposite Page

Report to

Shareholders

Designer Emery

Vincent Associates

Art Director

Garry Emery

Client

CRA Limited

German Contemporary

Graphics Exhibition Poster

Designers Annalese Cairis, Anthony

Ginns · Ginns Design Group Pty Ltd

Art Director Anthony Ginns

Illustrator A R Penck

Typographer Annalese Cairis

Client Museum of Contemporary Art

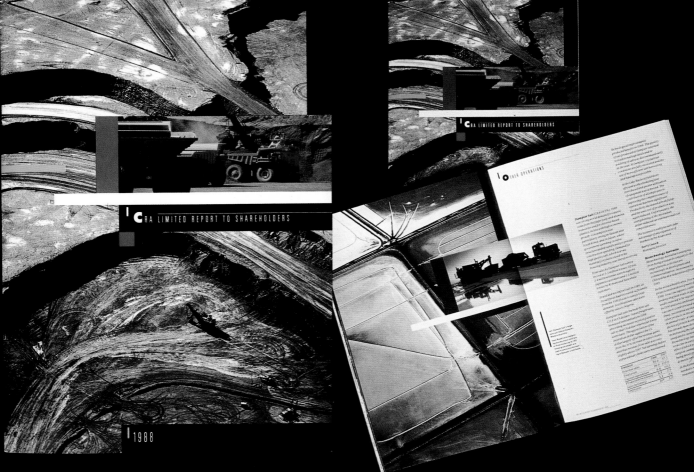

Graduate Exhibition Invitation

Designer Swinburne School of Design

Art Director John Bassani

Illustrator Thomas Arroquero

Typographer Swinburne Design Centre

Client Swinburne School of Design

Opposite Page

Self Promotion Designer Vince Engel

Geoff Brown Photography

Photographer Geoff Brown

Typographer FACE

Client Geoff Brown

Call for Entries Brochure

Designer Tanja Brjoc · Tanja Brjoc

Design **Typographer** Tanja Brjoc

Client National Print Awards

Opposite Page

Vic Fin Annual Report 1990

Designer Martin Wilson

Stuart Pettigrew Design

Art Director Stuart Pettigrew

Illustrator David Higgins

Client Victorian Public Authorities

Finance Agency

Calendar Designer John Nowland, Chris Ball

John Nowland Design **Client** Petaluma Wines

Opposite Page

Christmas Card Designer Keith Davis,

Gillian Allen · Cato Design Inc NSW

Art Director Keith Davis

Illustrators Various

Typographer Keith Davis, Gillian Allen

Client AMP

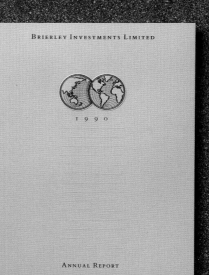

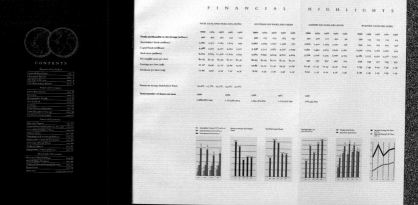

Playbox Programme

Designer Nigel Beechey · Cato Design Inc

Client Playbox Theatre

Opposite Page/Above

1990 Investment Company Annual Report

Designers Fay McAlpine, Ray Labone · Designworks

Photographers John Crawford, Ed Pritchard

Art Director Ray Labone **Illustrator** Donna Cross

Typographer Ray Labone **Client** Brierley Investments Limited

Paper Selector Designers Anna Cauchi, Anthony Ginns

Ginns Design Group Pty Ltd **Art Director** Anthony Ginns

Illustrator Drawing Book Studios **Typographer** Anna Cauchi

Client Mitchell Ross

Opposite Page

Corporate Profile

Designer

FHA Design

Client

FHA Design

Wedding Invitation

Designer Terry Dear · Ultra Graphics

Photographer Nicholas White

Client Terry & Kate Dear

Opposite Page

'Horizons' Club Resort Brochure

Designer Emery Vincent Associates

Art Director Garry Emery

Client NID Australia

Magazine Designer Billy Blue Group

Client Billy Blue Group

1988 Annual Report for Investment Bankers

Designer Ross Barr · Ross Barr & Associates Pty Ltd

Photographers Anthony Browell, Kraig Carlstrom

Art Director Ross Barr **Illustrator** Rosemary Webber

Typographer Ross Barr **Client** Schroders Australia Limited

Communication Graphics

Opposite Page

1989-1990 Annual Report

Designer Isabel Gaven Design Pty Limited

Illustrator Michael Golding

Typographer Isabel Gaven Design

Pty Limited **Client** NSW Department

of Sport, Recreation and Racing

Young Presidents Organisation

Invitation Designer Kuen Kam

Nelson Leong Art Direction & Design

Art Director Kuen Kam

Typographer Nelson Leong

Client Peter Metzner Event Management

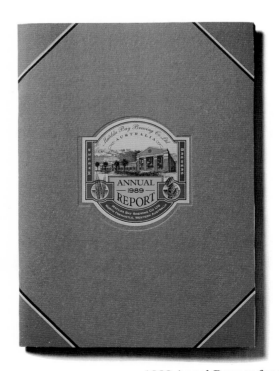

1989 Anual Report for Brewing Company

Designer Roland Butcher · Turner Design

Art Director Neil Turner **Illustrator** Danka Pradynski

Typographer Roland Butcher

Client Matilda Bay Brewing Company

Communication Graphics

NSW department of
Sport, Recreation and Racing

annual
report
1989-1990

DOMINION
MINING
LIMITED
ANNUAL
REPORT 1989

Opposite Page/Right

1989 Annual Report for Mining

Company **Designer** Anne Foster

Ross Barr & Associates Pty Ltd

Photographer Gerrit Fokkema

Art Director Ross Barr

Typographer Anne Foster

Client Dominion Mining Ltd

Cookbook **Designer** Peter Jeurgens · Professional Graphics

Photographer Rowan Fotheringham **Art Director** Jodi Lawton

Typographer Marcello Fulgenzi

Client Meat & Livestock Association

Christmas Party Invitations

Designer Mykl Pratt

Wood Pratt Wallace Design

Illustrator Wayne Harris

Client Australian Graphic

Design Association

Book Cover **Illustrator** Ned Culic

Designer Ned Culic · Ned Culic Design

Client Illustrators of Australia

Opposite Page

1988 Annual

Report for Media

Company

Designers

Elda Charous,

Greg Mackay

Kameruka

Design Group

Client

Northern Star

Holdings Limited

Building on the expertise developed during the coverage of the 1984 Los Angeles Olympics, Network TEN brought Australia the world's greatest sporting event – the 1988 Seoul Olympics. Two years in the planning, the coverage demonstrated the Network's commitment to quality broadcasting of important sporting events. More than 200 dedicated professionals made the trip to Seoul and, in combination with their colleagues in Australia, put to air more than 230 hours of Olympic coverage. The success of the telecast resulted in major ratings wins, a tribute to the contribution of all involved.

This expertise in sport led to Olympics organisers appointing Network TEN to cover the Yachting Regatta, one of the most technically difficult and demanding series of the Games. The Network coverage was distributed for use by broadcasters around the world. This approach to sport will continue to be a feature of the Network's coverage of events such as the Melbourne Cup, Rugby League, the Australian Indoor Tennis Championships, the Sydney-Hobart Yacht Race, the PGA Riverside Oaks and Australian Bicentennial Golf Classic.

Brochure for Financial Engineers

Designer Keith Davis, John Howe

Cato Design Inc NSW

Photographer Gerrit Fokkema

Art Director Keith Davis

Illustrator John Howe

Typographers Keith Davis, John Howe

Client The Optech Group

Opposite Page

Corporate Profile for Airline

Designer FHA Design

Photographer James Cant, RAAF

Client Ansett Technologies

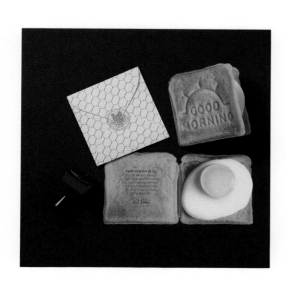

Self Promotion Sandwich

Designers Paul Nolan, Dennis Veal

Nolan Design

Photographer Andrew Houkamau

Illustrator John Morris **Copywriter**

David Heenan **Client** Paul Nolan

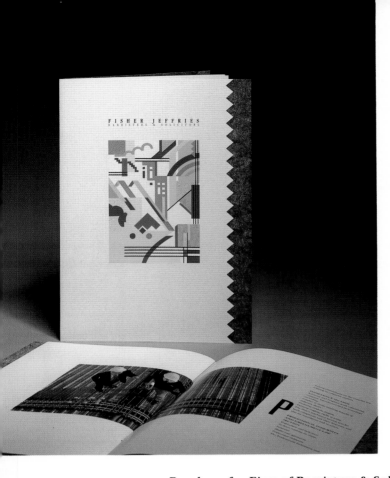

Opposite Page

Laminex

Invitation to

Launch Poster

Designer

Ken Cato

Cato Design Inc

Client

Laminex Industries

Brochure for Firm of Barristers & Solicitors

Designer Ian Kidd · Ian Kidd Design Pty Limited

Photographer Peter Fisher **Art Director** Ian Kidd

Illustrator Karin Seja **Typographer** Karin Seja

Client Fisher Jeffries

The Sydney Law School Foundation Invitation

Designer Kuen Kam · Nelson Leong Art Direction & Design

Art Directors Kuen Kam, Stephen Harrington

Typographer Kuen Kam **Client** Bridges Sharpe Consultants

you are
invited to
participate in

the australian launch of
the Laminex colour spectrum

colours that respond
to your specifications

the launch will reveal
our new colour range
together with other new
products and future
developments from
Laminex Industries

you are
invited to
participate in

the australian launch of
the Laminex colour spectrum

colours that respond
to your specifications

the launch will reveal
our new colour range
together with other new
products and future
developments from
Laminex Industries

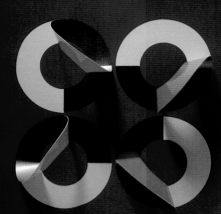

you are
invited to
participate in

the australian launch of
the Laminex colour spectrum

colours that respond
to your specifications

the launch will reveal
our new colour range
together with other new
products and future
developments from
Laminex Industries

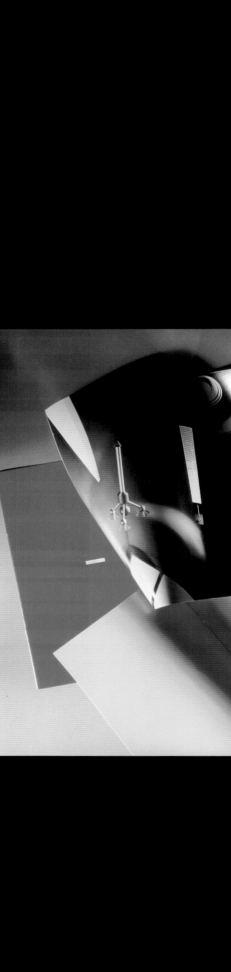

Programme

Designer Jeff Thornton · Cato Design Inc

Client The Australian Ballet

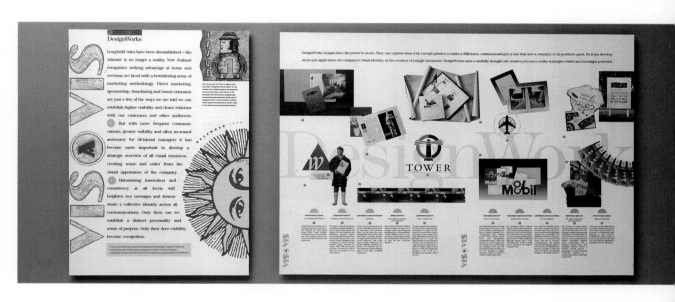

Promotional Brochure Designer Grant Alexander · Designworks

Photographer Sal Criscillo **Art Director** Grant Alexander

Typographer Grant Alexander **Client** Designworks

Opposite Page

Stationery Products Designers Peter Roband,

Peter Haythornthwaite · Peter Haythornthwaite Design

Photographers Bill Nichol, Neil Liversedge

Art Director Peter Haythornthwaite

Typographer Peter Roband

Client Artifakts Designs Limited

Opposite Page

Cafe Bar Products Folder

Designers Peter Finlay, Anthony Ginns

Ginns Design Group Pty Ltd

Art Director Anthony Ginns

Illustrator Peter Finlay

Typographer Peter Finlay

Client The Armory

Corporate Profile Designer Cato Design Inc

Client Melbourne International Festival Committee

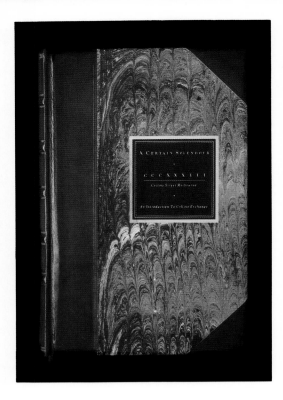

'A Certain Splendor'

Designer Emery Vincent Associates

Art Director Garry Emery

Client Becton Corporation

Opposite Page

Hotel Brochure Designer FHA Design

Photographer James Cant,

Client Rydges Hotel Group

Self Promotional Booklet

Designer Anne Foster · Ross Barr & Associates Pty Ltd

Art Director Ross Barr **Illustrator** Anne Foster

Typographer Anne Foster **Client** Ross Barr & Associates Pty Ltd

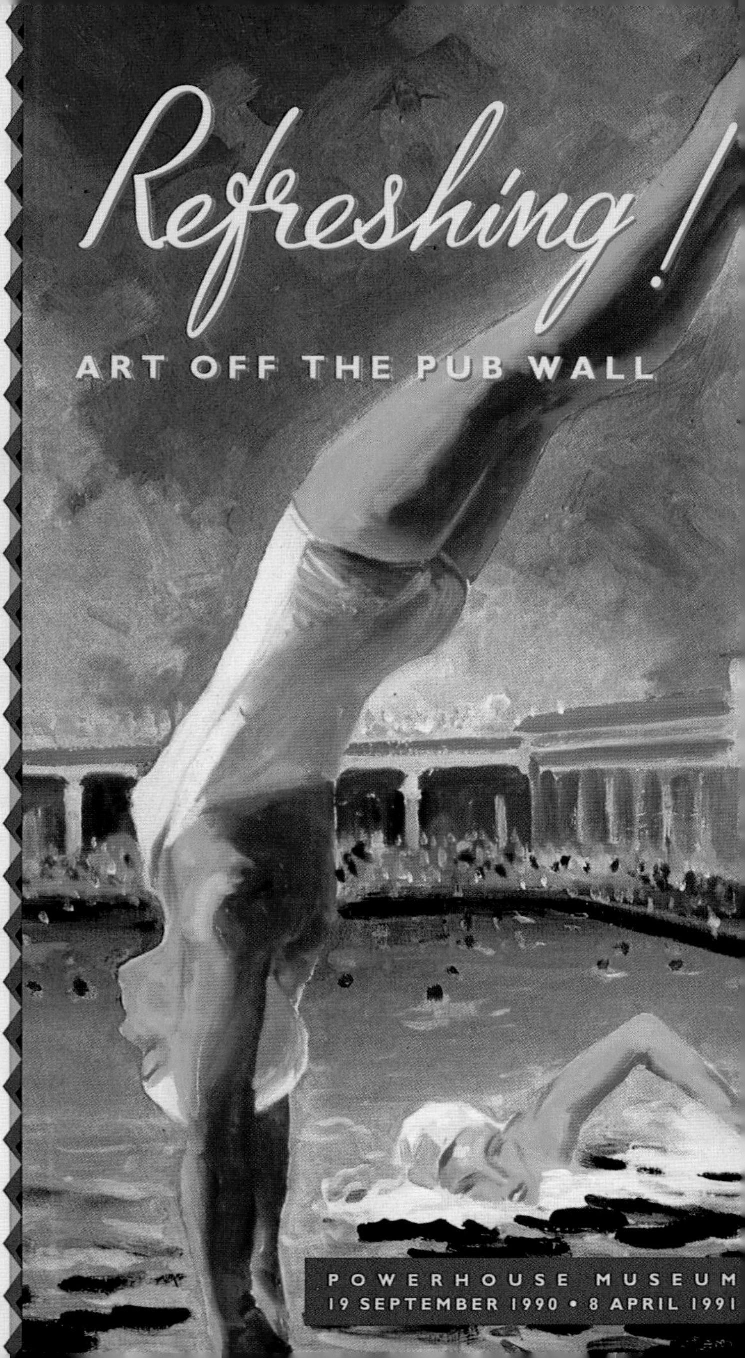

Refreshing!

ART OFF THE PUB WALL

POWERHOUSE MUSEUM
LEVEL 5 • 500 HARRIS ST
ULTIMO • OPEN 10AM–5PM
DAILY • CLOSED CHRISTMAS
DAY AND GOOD FRIDAY
• ADMISSION FREE •

POWERHOUSE MUSEUM
19 SEPTEMBER 1990 • 8 APRIL 1991

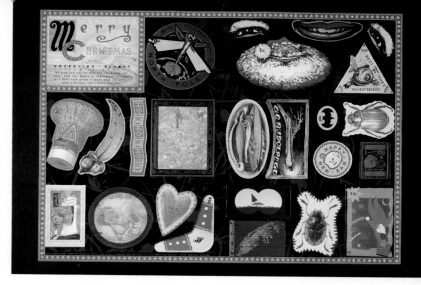

Opposite Page

Posters and Book 'Art off the Pub Wall'

Designer Colin Rowan

Powerhouse Museum

Photographers Peter Garrett,

Geof Frien, Penelope Clay

Art Director Colin Rowan

Typographer Colin Rowan

Self Promotion Christmas Card

Designer Andrew Hook

Cozzolino/Ellett Design D'Vision

Art Director Mimmo Cozzolino

Illustrators Andrew Hook,

Geoff Kelly, Darren Ledwich

Typographer Andrew Hook

Client Cozzolino/Ellett Design D'Vision

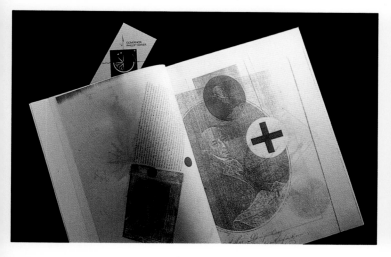

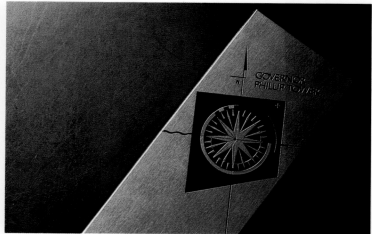

Governor Phillip Tower **Designer** Emery Vincent Associates

Art Director Garry Emery **Client** State Authority

Superannuation Board of NSW

Opposite Page

Barcelona Olympics Brochure

Designers Peter Debeer, David Duvall

Debeer Adams Associates

Typographer Online Design

Client Television New Zealand

Corporate Profile

Designer FHA Design

Photographer Mark Chew

Client Southern Printing

Structure Spanning Time Designers Suzie Zezula, Jason
Sealey, Fiona Mahon, Design Dept - Phillip Institute of
Technology **Photographer** Tim Griffith **Art Directors** Enzo
Conti, Lauren Murray **Illustrators** Robert Godino, Archie
Bourtsoz, Campbell Paton **Typographers** Suzie Zezula,
Jason Sealey **Client** Design Department, Phillip
Institute of Technology

Communication Graphics

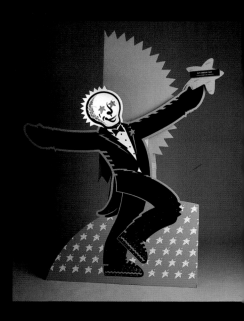

Self Promotion Christmas Card

Designer Brian Nelson · The Art of Style

Client Suters Architect Snell

1989 Annual Report for Mining

Company Designer Anne Foster

Ross Barr & Associates Pty Ltd

Photographer Gerrit Fokkema

Art Director Ross Barr

Typographer Anne Foster

Client Placer Pacific Limited

Opposite Page

MADC Awards 1991 Designer Philip Ellett

Cozzolino/Ellett Design D'Vision

Art Director Mimmo Cozzolino

Illustrators Philip Ellett, Carmel Raccosta

Typographer Philip Ellett

Client Melbourne Art Directors Club Awards

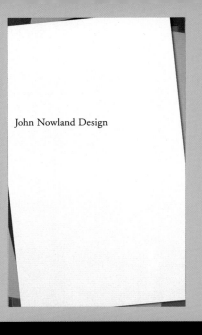

John Nowland Design

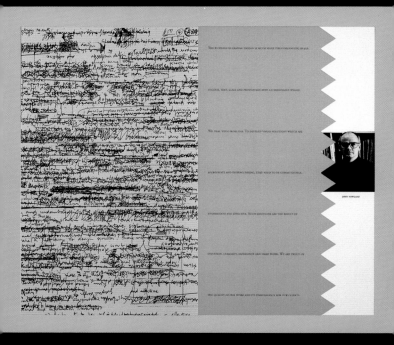

Opposite Page

Self Promotion Brochure

Designer John Nowland, Chris Ball

John Nowland Design

Calendar 1991 Designer David Lancashire

David Lancashire Design **Photographer** Angie Heinl

Client Coogi Australia

Self Promotional Calendar Designer FHA Design

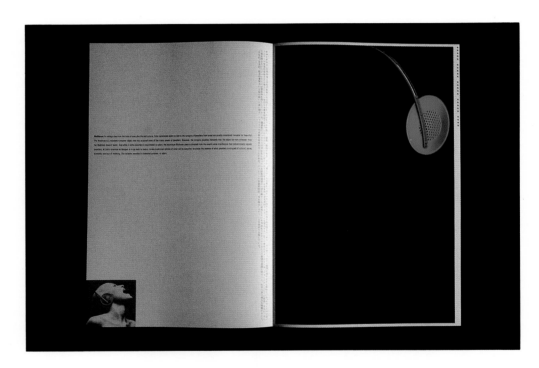

'**Workshop 3000**' **Designer** Emery Vincent Associates

Photographer Kate Gollings **Art Director** Garry Emery

Client Susan Cohn, Workshop 3000

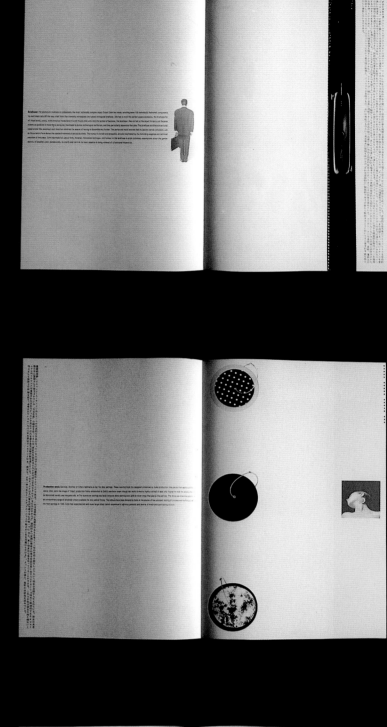

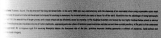

Opposite Page

Catalogue for Typesetters

Designer Lee Callister

Lee Callister Design

Typographer Peter Berney

Client Berney Studios

Services Profile for Corporate Superannuation

Fund Managers Designer Andrew Lam-Po-Tang

Lam-Po-Tang & Co Pty Limited **Photographer** Urs Buhlman

Client Capita Benefits Planning

LEEUWIN
ESTATE
WESTERN AUSTRALIA

DALTON
FINE PAPER

DESIGN, ART DIRECTION AND COPYWRITING BY DAVID LANCASHIRE DESIGN. PAINTING BY DAVID LANCASHIRE. SEPARATIONS BY SHOW-ADS COLOUR CENTRE. PRINTED BY FRANK DANIELS PTY LTD PERTH ON A ROLAND RECORD RFK 50 PRESS.

THE Dalton
SELECTION OF
AUSTRALIAN
WINERIES

PETALUMA
WINES
SOUTH AUSTRALIA

DALTON

TULLOCH
WINES
NEW SOUTH WALES

DALTON

Opposite Page

Wine Posters

Designer David Lancashire

David Lancashire Design

Art Director David Lancashire

Illustrators D Lancashire, D Pryce,

A Chiappin, P Freeman

Typographer Godfrey Fawcetr

Client Dalton Fine Papers

Range of Menu Designs for Hotel Designer Annette Harcus

Annette Harcus Design **Illustrators** Annette Harcus,

Melinda Dudley **Client** The Oakford-Melbourne

Christmas Card

Designer John Nowland, Brenton Hill · John Nowland Design

Client Australian Graphic Design Association

Opposite Page

Paper Sample Book for Paper

Merchants Designers Anthony Ginns,

Anna Cauchi · Ginns Design

Group Pty Ltd **Art Director** Anthony

Ginns **Illustrator** Collin Mennell

Typographer Anna Cauchi

Client Mitchell Ross Paper

1989 Annual Report Designer Kajetan M Fiedorowicz

Kajetan Design Group **Photographer** Philip O Korczynski

Art Director Kajetan M Fiedorowicz **Illustrator** Michael Jarosz

Typographer Delmont Typography Pty Limited

Client The University of Melbourne

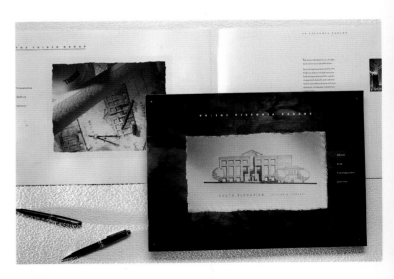

Property Brochure

Designer FHA Design

Photographer Tat-Ming Yu

Client Triden Properties Limited

Communication Graphics

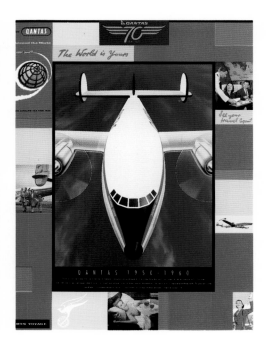

Opposite Page

Corporate Profile for Supplier &

Installers of Turf Management Systems

Designer David Roffey

David Roffey Design

Photographer Kraig Carlstrom

Client Sports Turf Dynamics

70th Anniversary

Posters for Airline

Designers Hans Hulsbosch,

Mark Tucker · Hulsbosch Pty Ltd

Photographer John Love

Illustrators Otto and Chris

Client Qantas Airways Limited

Communication Graphics

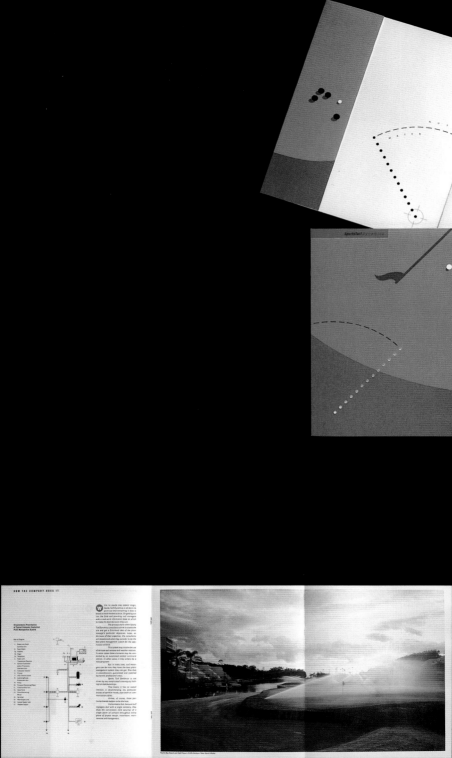

Facific Bay Resort and Golf Resort, Coffs Harbour, New South Wales.

Opposite Page

1990 Annual Report

Designers Mark Adams, Peter Debeer

Debeer Adams Associates

Typographer Artspec

Client Telecom Corporation

of New Zealand

'Charisma' Brochure

Designer Emery Vincent Associates

Art Director Garry Emery

Client Charisma Furniture

Restaurant Collateral

Designer FHA Design

Client Hyatt On Collins

Opposite Page

Personal Action

Guide to the Future

Designer Emery

Vincent Associates

Art Director Garry

Emery

Client Commission

for the Future

FIRST EDITION 1989 $3.50

ON TRANSPORT

The major cause of the worsening greenhouse effect is the
increasing level of carbon dioxide in the atmosphere - now
25 per cent higher than it was at the beginning of the
Industrial Revolution.

The burning of fossil fuels (coal, oil, petroleum and gas)
by motor vehicles and for electricity generation causes
around 85 per cent of this carbon dioxide build-up.

Motor vehicles are also the biggest source of air pollution
in our cities, adding carbon monoxide, unburned hydrocarbon
and oxides of nitrogen to the air we breathe.

ACTIONS

- Wherever possible, reduce your car use: travel by public
  transport more, cycle or walk.
- If you must travel to work by car, try to arrange a car pool
  with your friends.
- Buy bicycles for the whole family, and use them wherever
  possible instead of the family car.
- Ask your local council to construct bicycle paths in
  appropriate places, if they are not already there.
- Encourage the use of bicycles in your city or town. Ask for
  secure bicycle parking to be provided at train and bus
  stations, and for facilities to be installed so that
  bicycles can be carried on public transport.
- Shop locally and walk to the shops to buy household goods.
- Drive an energy efficient car, and have it serviced and
  tuned regularly. Make sure the car's pollution control
  devices are also serviced. (14)
- Drive smoothly and obey speed laws.
- Don't let your car idle unnecessarily. Switch off your
  engine when in a traffic jam.
- Don't buy a car with air conditioning.
- If you already have car air conditioning, try not to use it
  unless absolutely necessary.
- Keep your car air conditioner maintained to prevent the
  leaking of CFCs from the seals, and ask your service station
  to use CFC recovery equipment during air conditioning
  repairs.
- Don't carry unnecessary loads in the car boot, and don't
  overfill the petrol tank.

CROSSING

12

Corporate Identity

Freelance Creative Service Corporate Identity

Designers Philip Ellett, Carmel Raccosta · Cozzolino

Ellett Design D'Vision **Art Director** Mimmo Cozzolino

Illustrator Philip Ellett **Typographers** Philip Ellett, Carmel

Raccosta **Client** The Talent Store

Opposite Page/Above

Corporate Programme for Rottnest

Lodge Designer Ken Cato

Cato Design Inc

Illustrator Kim Roberts-Smith

Client Dallhold Investments

Opposite Page

Below

Corporate

Identity for

Fruniture

Manufacturer

Designer

Emery Vincent

Associates

Art Director

Garry Emery

Client Carmen

Furniture

(Sales) Pty Ltd

Earth Sun Studios Corporate Identity

Designer David Lancashire · David Lancashire Design

Client Jill Robin-Downes

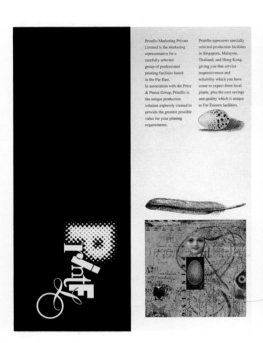

Printflo Marketing Private Limited is the marketing representative for a carefully selected group of professional printing facilities based in the Far East.
In association with the Price & Pierce Group, Printflo is the unique production solution expressly created to provide the greatest possible value for your printing requirements.

Printflo represents specially selected production facilities in Singapore, Malaysia, Thailand, and Hong Kong, giving you that service responsiveness and reliability which you have come to expect from local plants, plus the cost savings and quality which is unique to Far Eastern facilities.

Logistics management, of every minute detail, is a core Printflo strength.
Our customer service staff communicates on your behalf, managing and coordinating your project each and every step of the way from on-sight press checks to on-time delivery.
At Printflo, strict attention to details is more than a maxim, it is a constant performance standard.

Printflo, professional coordination of all logistics.

Opportunity is that blending of time and conditions that most favor the attainment of goals. If your Company's printing goals include cost effective, reliable and on-schedule service plus the highest quality production, the time to call Printflo is now.

Give us the opportunity and we will prove that Printflo is the production solution which provides the greatest possible value for your printing dollar.
With our staff at your side and on the site, we will deliver your specific requirements with precision.

Printflo, ready for you to seize the opportunity.

Printflo Marketing
Private Limited
250 North Bridge Road
#12-02 Raffles City Tower
Singapore 0617
Telephone 65 339 4311
Facsimile 65 339 3668

Printflo Marketing Limited
Eight Stamford Forum
P O Box 971 Stamford
Connecticut 00904
United States of America
Telephone 1 203 378 7000
Facsimile 1 203 967 3651

Identity Programme Planning & Development Consultants

Designer Emery Vincent Associates **Art Director** Garry Emery

Client Ratio Consultants Pty Ltd

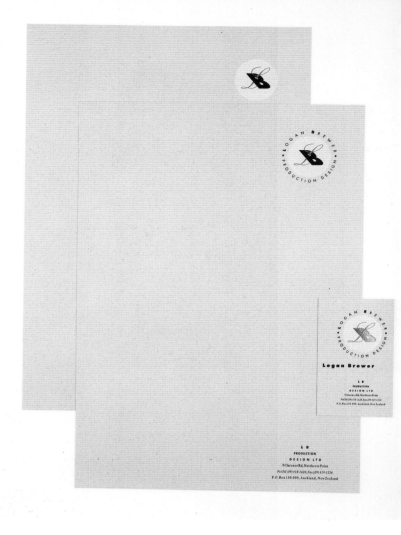

Turnaround time is a key factor in all projects. At Printflo, we know that time, like money, must be budgeted for maximum efficiency. As time requirements are unique for each project, Printflo works with you to manage turnaround time according to your schedule.

Timely delivery coupled with cost-efficiency and quality is our chief concern. When it comes to turnaround, Printflo delivers on time, every time!

Printflo, the timely solution.

Corporate Identity Programe

Designer Phil O'Reilly

Phil O'Reilly Design Ltd

Typographer Jill McNaughton

Client L B Production Design

Opposite Page/Above

Stationery Range   Designer Ken Cato · Cato Design Inc

Client Printflo Marketing Limited

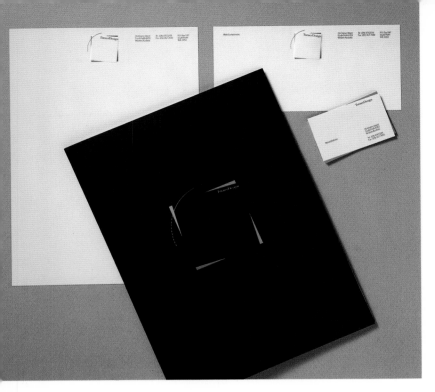

Corporate Identity Programme

Designer Roland Butcher · Turner Design

Art Director Neil Turner

Client Turner Design

Stationery Range

Designer

Anne Barton

Barton Wendt

Design

Art Director Anne

Barton

Illustrator

Nigel Buchanan

Typographer

Anne Barton

Client

Advocado Pty Ltd

Fashion Company Stationery Range

Designers Stephanie Martin, Annette Harcus · Annette Harcus

Design **Retoucher** Vanessa Yeo **Typographer** Stephanie Martin

Client Cue Design Pty Ltd

Advocado

To:

Date:

Invoice Number:

Client:

Order Number:

Your Job Number:

My Job Number:

Job Description:

INVOICE

Advocado
Pty Ltd
2/72
Avenue
Road
Mosman
NSW
2088
Australia
Telephone
(02)
9600 02804
Facsimile
(02)
9600 53528

Advocado Pty Ltd
2/72 Avenue Road
Mosman NSW 2088
Australia
Telephone (02) 9600 02804
Facsimile (02) 9600 53528

ANNIE MEHRA • *Copywriter*

Advocado

Advocado
Pty Ltd
2/72
Avenue
Road
Mosman
NSW
2088
Australia
Telephone
(02)
9600 02804
Facsimile
(02)
9600 53528

With Compliments

ANNIE MEHRA • *Copywriter*

Total:

Terms: 30 days nett
Any claims regarding this invoice must be made within fourteen days from date of invoice.

MEHRA • *Copywriter*

Compass

Stationery Range Designers Anne
Barton, Bryant Wendt · Barton Wendt
Design **Client** Northbeach

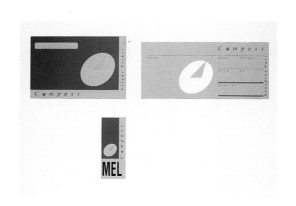

Opposite Page/Above

Corporate Identity for Airline Designer Brian Sadgrove

Brian Sadgrove & Associates **Client** Compass Airlines

Melbourne Olympic Candidature

Corporate Programme

Designer Ken Cato · Cato Design Inc

Client The Melbourne Olympic

Candidature 1996

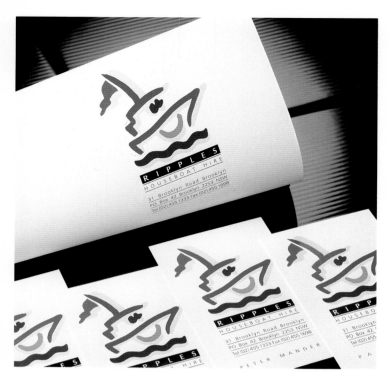

Ripples Houseboat Hire Corporate

Identity Designer Pam Connelly

Icarus Industrial Design Pty Ltd

Art Director David Robertson

Illustrator Pam Connelly

Typographer Pam Connelly

Client Ripples Houseboat Hire

Opposite Page

Corporate

Identity for

Architecture &

Planning

Development Co

Designer Emery

Vincent Associates

Art Director

Garry Emery

Client Ashton

Raggatt McDougall

Architects

Corporate

Identity for

Architects

Designer Emery

Vincent Associates

Art Director

Garry Emery

Client Denton

Corker Marshall

Pty Ltd

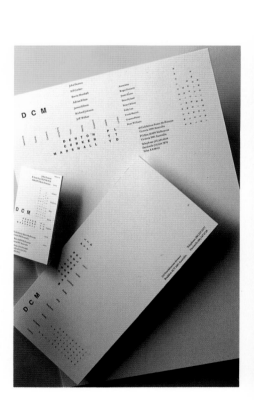

Ashton   Raggatt   McDougall

Ashton Raggatt McDougall

Architecture

Invitation

You are invited
to attend
pre-dinner drinks,
to celebrate
the launch of
Ashton Raggatt McDougall Pty Ltd

The evening
will be introduced by
Professor
Peter McIntyre AO
and addressed
by Mr Gary Neil,
an/Principal of
ARM

Time: 5.30 to 7.30 pm
Date: Wednesday
16 November
LOCATION
The Sophia Restaurant
(Melbourne reference 2F - 40)
Deck 3
Southbank Food Wall
Terrace on
Normanby Road
Ample parking
is available adjacent
to the restaurant

RSVP 10 November
to Ann on (03) 7100

Opposite Page

Corporate Identity for Countrylink

Holidays Designers Anthony Ginns,

Tim Lyddon · Ginns Design

Group Pty Ltd

Art Director Anthony Ginns

Typographer Tim Lyddon

Client Countrylink

Corporate Identity for Printing Company

Designer Alison Hulett · Eymont Kin-Yee Design

Client Paddington Print

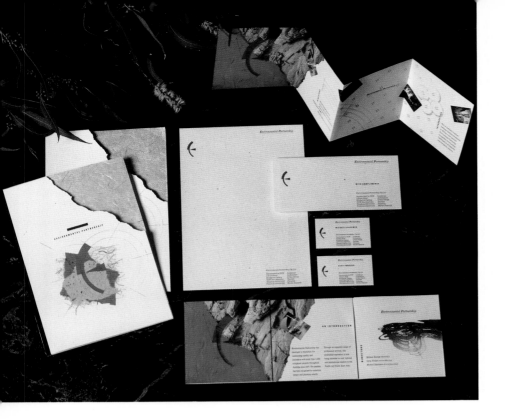

Stationery Range and Promotions

Designers Graham Rendoth, Carlos
Camacho · Reno Visual Communications

Client Environmental Partnership Pty Ltd

Corporate Identity for Framing

Specialist Designer Emery Vincent

Associates **Art Director** Garry Emery

Client Fini Frames

Stationery Range Designer Mykl Pratt · Wood

Pratt Wallace Design **Illustrator** Wayne Harris

Client Headlands on Broken Bay

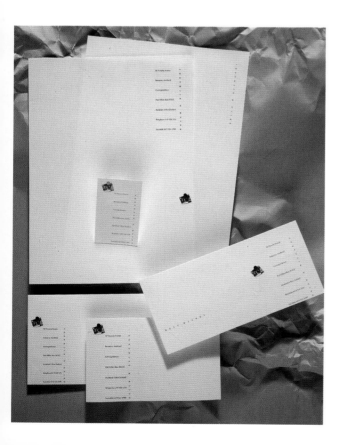

Stationery Range Designers Peter Haythornthwaite,

Rodney Abbot · Peter Haythornthwaite Design

Art Director Peter Haythornthwaite **Illustrator** Vermeer

Typographers Peter Haythornthwaite, Rodney Abbot

Client Brian Richards

Visual Identity for Vaucluse House

Tea-Rooms Designer Annette Harcus

Annette Harcus Design

Client John Guthrie

Opposite Page

The Bryson Hotel

Collateral

Designer

FHA Design

Client Rydges

Hotel Group

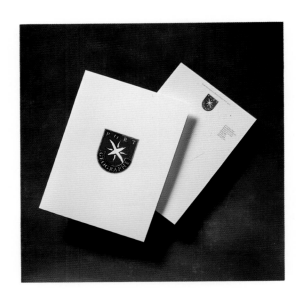

Port Geographe Marina Development

Designer Roland Butcher · Turner Design

Art Director Neil Turner

Illustrator Mary Mason

Typographer Roland Butcher

Client Port Geographe

Development Pty Ltd

Corporate Identity

Dear Guest,
We noticed that you
out tonight and ther
turndown service.
Please call Houseke
you require service
to at the earliest po

Sincerely
Your Executive Hou

PLEASE MAKE

PRIVACY REQUESTED

The Pumphouse Hotel Corporate

Identity Designer Philip Ellett

Cozzolino Ellett Design D'Vision

Art Director Mimmo Cozzolino

Illustrator Geoff Kelly

Typographer Philip Ellett

Client The Pumphouse Hotel

Opposite Page

Presentation to World Economic

Forum - Davos 1990 Designers Russell

Springham, Andrew Stumpfel · Springham

Design Photographer Richard

Woldendorp Client Sattler & Associates

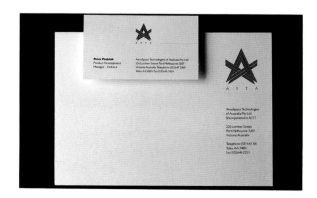

Corporate Identity Programme

Designer Emery Vincent Associates

Art Director Garry Emery

Client Aerospacetechnologies of Australia

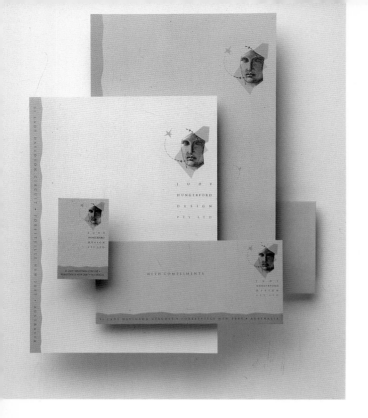

Stationery Range & Corporate Identity

Programme Designer Judy Hungerford

Judy Hungerford Design Pty Ltd

Illustrator Tony Pyrzakowski

Client Judy Hungerford Design Pty Ltd

Corporate Identity for Photographics Company

Designer Ian Kidd · Ian Kidd Design Pty Ltd

Illustrator Karin Seja **Client** Van Elsen Photographics Pty Ltd

Restaurant Stationery

Designer FHA Design

Client Sweetwater Restaurant

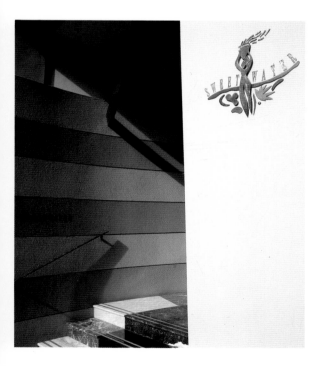

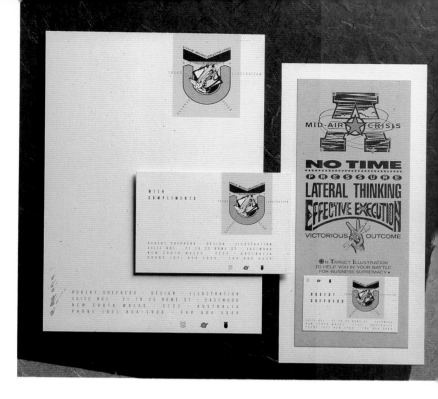

Opposite Page

Identity for Shipping Company

Designers Peter Finlay, Anthony Ginns

Ginns Design Group Pty Ltd

Art Director Anthony Ginns

Illustrator Drawing Book Studios

Typographer Peter Finlay

Client Seaport Shipping

Stationery Range

Designer Robert Shepherd

Robert Shepherd Design Illustration

Television Corporate Identity

Designers Ian Ryder, Rob Stevenson

Ian Kennon Advertising

Art Directors Ian Ryder, Rob Stevenson

Typographers David Rust, Smith & Miles

Client ABC Television

Corporate Identity

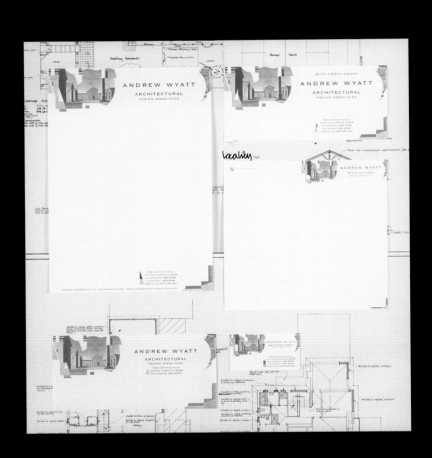

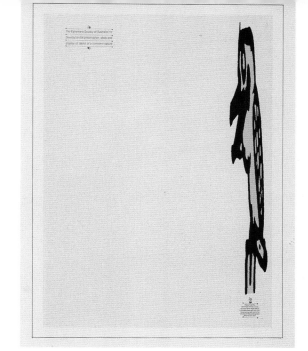

Opposite Page

Andrew Wyatt Corporate Identity

Designer Kevin Wilkins · Siren

Client Andrew Wyatt Architectural

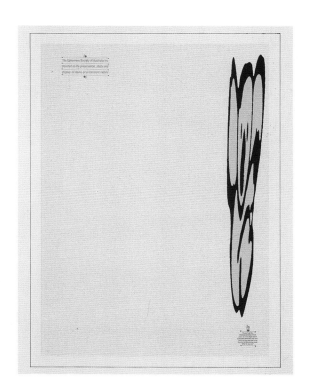

Ephemera Letterheads Designer Mimmo Cozzolino

Cozzolino Ellett Design D'Vision

Illustrator Mimmo Cozzolino

Typographers Mimmo Cozzolino, Anna Day

Client The Ephemera Society of Australia Inc

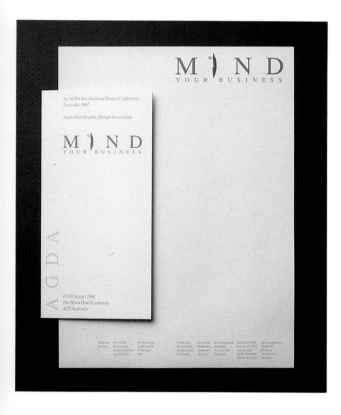

Mind Your Business Logotype

Designer Brian Sadgrove · Brian Sadgrove

& Associates **Client** Australian Graphic

Design Association

Opposite Page

Corporate Identity Programme Designer Andrew Lam-Po

Tang · Lam-Po-Tang & Co Pty Ltd **Client** Belvoir St Theatre

BELVOIR

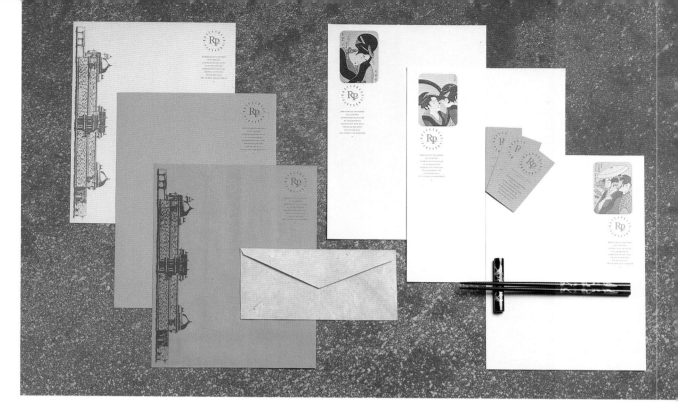

Asian Restaurants Stationery Range

Designer Kristen Thieme · Annette Harcus Design

Art Director Trevor Crump **Typographer** Kristen Thieme

Client Restaurant Partners Pty Ltd

Opposite Page/Below

Corporate Programme for

Manufacturing Company

Designer Ken Cato · Cato Design Inc

Client Laminex Industries

Stationery Range for Printing Company

Designer Ken Cato · Cato Design Inc

Client Vega Press Pty Ltd

Identity for Industrial Design Company

Designers Anthony Ginns, Annalese Cairis · Ginns Design

Group Pty Ltd **Art Director** Anthony Ginns

Typographer Anthony Ginns **Client** KWA Design Group

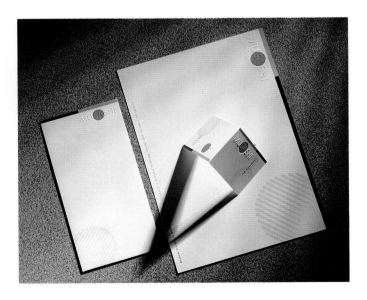

Corporate Identity and Stationery Designer Wayne Rankin

Rankin Bevers Design **Client** Musashi

Stationery Range Designer FHA Design

Photographer Brendan Beacon **Art Director** FHA Design,

Lisa Moore **Client** Laine Furnishings

Melbourne Spoleto Festival

September 14 to 30 1989

Melbourne Spoleto Festival Identity

Programme

Designer Ken Cato · Cato Design Inc

Client Melbourne Spoleto Festival

Committee

MELBOURNE SPOLETO FESTIVAL

BOURNE SPOLETO FESTIVAL

MELBOURNE
SPOLETO
FESTIVAL

QUALITY IMAGES

Printers Identity

Designers Anthony Ginns, Anna Cauchi

Ginns Design Group Pty Ltd

Art Director Anthony Ginns

Typographer Anna Cauchi

Client Quality Images

Opposite Page

Stationery Range

for Architectural

Company

Designer

Brian Nelson

The Art of Style

Client Suters

Architect Snell

Stationery Corporate Identity Designers Mary Davy, Penny

Gillette · Mary Davy Design **Client** Pindara Developments

Corporate Identity

Visual Identity for 'The Oriental' Asian Restaurant

Designer Annette Harcus · Annette Harcus Design

Client Restaurant Partners

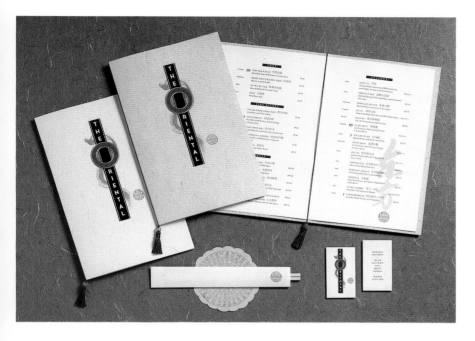

Corporate

Identity & Manual

Designer Ian Kidd

Ian Kidd Design

Pty Ltd

Typographer

Donna Merrett

Client Adelaide

Entertainment

Centre

Opposite Page

Stationery Range

Designer Mykl Pratt · Wood Pratt

Wallace Design

Illustrator Wayne Haris

Client Bear Uno Pty Ltd

Stationery Range for Insurance Underwriters

Designer FHA Design **Client** Heath Fielding Australia

Opposite Page/Above

Logotype Designer Graham Rendoth

Reno Visual Communications

Client NSW Department of School

Education

Identity for Swimwear Manufacturer

Designers Peter Finlay, Anthony Ginns

Ginns Design Group Pty Ltd

Art Director Anthony Ginns

Typographer Peter Finlay

Client Desino

Opposite Page

Stationery/Brochure Corporate

Identity Designer Carol Whittaker

Tony Masters Design Pty Ltd

Photographer Willem Rethmeier

Art Director Carol Whittaker

Typographer Carol Whittaker

Client D H Gibson Pty Ltd

MODA

GENUA

MARE

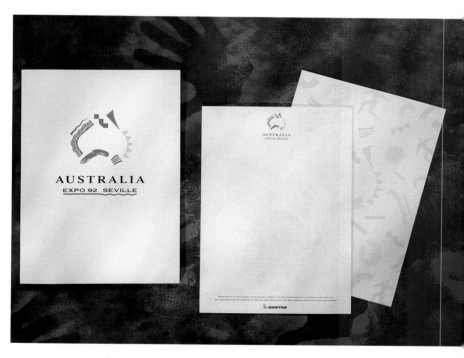

Stationery Range for Australian

Pavilion at Expo '92 Seville

Designer FHA Design

Client Dept of Arts, Sport, Environment,

Tourism & Territories

Corporate Identity

Packaging

Angove's

Winemaker's

Limited Edition

Designer

Barrie Tucker

Barrie Tucker

Design Pty Ltd

Typographer

Barrie Tucker,

Elizabeth Schlooz

Art Director

Barrie Tucker

Illustrator

Barrie Tucker

Client

Angove's Pty Ltd

Survival Shiraz **Designer** David Lancashire

David Lancashire Design **Client** David Lancashire

Padthaway Estate

Designers Barrie Tucker, Jody Tucker

Barrie Tucker Design Pty Limited

Art Director Barrie Tucker

Illustrator Jody Tucker

Typographer Jody Tucker

Client Padthaway Estate

Showclub – World of Wonders **Designer** Mark Denning
Mark Denning Graphic Design **Client** Virgin Records

Sylvain Fessy Beaujolais Nouveau
Designers Barrie Tucker, Luci
Giannettilio · Barrie Tucker
Design Pty Ltd **Art Director** Barrie
Tucker **Illustrator** Barrie Tucker
Typographers Barrie Tucker, Elizabeth
Schlooz **Client** Negociants International

Self Promotion

Designer Roland Butcher · Turner Design

Art Director Neil Turner

Illustrator Roland Butcher

Typographer Roland Butcher

Client Turner Design

Opposite Page

South Cape Brie

Wrapper

Designer

Nigel Beechey

Cato Design Inc

Client Butterfields

Mountadam - The Red

Designers Barrie Tucker, Jody Tucker

Barrie Tucker Design Pty Ltd

Art Director Barrie Tucker

Typographers Barrie Tucker, Jody

Tucker Client David & Adam

Wynn Pty Limited

Yalumba Ten Year Old Port Designers Barrie Tucker,

Elizabeth Schlooz · Barrie Tucker Design Pty Ltd

Art Director Barrie Tucker **Typographers** Elizabeth Schlooz,

Paul Dowell **Client** S Smith & Son

Manor House Labels Designer Lucy
Walker · Andrew Lewis & Company
Art Director Andrew Lewis
Illustrators Lucy Walker, John Gittoes
Typographer Lucy Walker
Client Masterfoods of Australia Pty Ltd

Portmans Carry Bag
Designer Chris Perks · Cato Design Inc
Client Portmans Consolidated
Pty Limited

Devil's Lair Wine Label **Designer** Roland Butcher
Turner Design **Art Director** Neil Turner **Illustrators** Roland
Butcher, Malcolm Lindsay **Typographer** Roland Butcher
Client Devil's Lair Wines

Opposite Page

Pierre Beuchet

Beaujolais

Villages

Designer

Barrie Tucker

Barrie Tucker

Design Pty Limited

Art Director

Barrie Tucker

Illustrator

Vi Wilson

Typographers

Paul Dowell, Barrie

Tucker

Client S Smith

& Son

Target Cotton Hipster Label
Designer Brian Sadgrove · Brian Sadgrove
& Associates **Client** Holeproof

Rymill Wine Labels **Designer** Brian
Sadgrove · Brian Sadgrove & Associates
Client Rymill Wines

Campbell's Real Stock Packs

Designer Chris Perks · Cato Design Inc

Client Campbell's Australasia

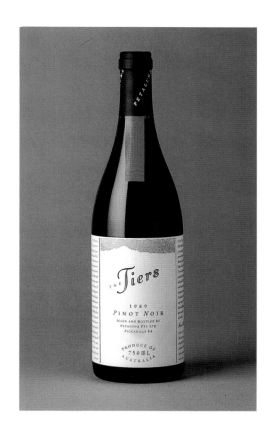

Opposite Page

Prelude Wine

Labels

Designer

Nigel Beechey

Cato Design Inc

Client Leeuwin

Estate Winery

Tiers Pinot Noir

Designers John Nowland, Brenton Hill

John Nowland Design **Client** Petaluma

Wines

Opposite Page/Above

Perth City Foreshore Urban Design

Competition Designers K J Wohlnick, M

R Barcham, J Adamson · Nex Design Group

Pty Ltd **Art Director** K J Wohlnick

Illustrator K J Wohlnick

Client State Government of W A & Council

of City of Perth

Ironbrew Designer Roland Butcher

Turner Design **Art Director** Neil Turner

Illustrator Danka Pradynski

Typographer Roland Butcher

Client Matilda Bay Brewing Company

Opposite Page

Morris of Rutherglen Fortifieds

Designers Barrie Tucker, Jody Tucker

Barrie Tucker Design Pty Ltd

Art Director Barrie Tucker

Illustrators Jody Tucker, Dover

Typographer Jody Tucker

Client Morris Wines Pty Limited

Cobaw Ridge Wine Labels

Designer Brian Sadgrove · Brian Sadgrove

& Associates **Client** Cobaw Ridge Winery

Instant Starch Pack

Designer Raymond Falzon

TKR Graphics **Client** Samuel Taylor

LIQUEUR
MUSCAT

MORRIS of RUTHERGLEN

LIQUEUR
MUSCAT

MORRIS of RUTHERGLEN

Wedding Invitation Designer FHA Design

Client Margaret Dengate

Howarth Wine Labels Designers John

Nowland, Brenton Hill · John Nowland

Design Client Jim Howarth

Opposite Page

Orlando

Steingarten Rhine

Riesling

Designer

Barrie Tucker

Barrie Tucker

Design Pty Ltd

Art Director

Barrie Tucker

Typographers

Barrie Tucker,

Elizabeth Schlooz

Client

G Gramp & Sons

Mandarin Oriental Guest Room Amenities

Designer Erin Corlette · Corlette Design

Client Watermen Worldwide

Sarsi Diet Light Can

Designer Ken Cato · Cato Design Inc

Client Fraser & Neave (Singapore)

Pte Ltd

Hanshin Shopping Bags

Designer Chris Perks · Cato Design Inc **Client** Hanshin

Packaging

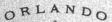

ORLANDO

STEINGARTEN®

RHINE RIESLING

Vintage 1988

GRAMP & SONS
G'PPY LTD
ROWLAND FLAT
SOUTH AUSTRALIA

Opposite Page

Pinot Noir Blush

Wine Label

Designer

Mark Adams

Debeer Adams

Associates

Typographer

Jacobsons

Client

Lincoln Vineyards

Colour Guide For Tapestry Yarns

Designer Wayne Rankin

Rankin Bevers Design

Art Director Livio Andolfatto

Client Victorian Tapestry Workshop

Carry Bag Designer Ken Done

Done Art & Design

Client Done Art & Design

Cockatoo Lager Designer Chris Perks

Cato Design Inc **Client** Bond Corporation

Martin Pedersen Wine Pack Designer Dennis Veal

Dennis Veal Design **Illustrator** Phil Ellett

Client Australian Graphic Design Association/Tomasetti

Pinball Labels

Designers Annette Harcus, Stephanie
Martin · Annette Harcus Design
Illustrators Melinda Dudley, Annette
Harcus, Vanessa Yeo
Typographer Annette Harcus
Client Sunshine Clothing Company

Moorodduc Wines Label
Designer Brian Sadgrove
Brian Sadgrove & Associates
Client Moorodduc Wines

RED ✦ RED

THE BIBLE TELLS US "GO TO THE ANT,
CONSIDER HER WAYS AND BE WISE", WITH
THIS IN MIND WE RECOMMEND YOU GO TO
THE RED ANT RED AND ENJOY. MERRY
CHRISTMAS AND A PEACEFUL NEW YEAR TO
YOU AND YOURS FROM DAVID LANCASHIRE
DESIGN. RED ANT RED WAS SPECIALLY
BOTTLED BY CAMPBELLS OF RUTHERGLEN.

1986
CABERNET

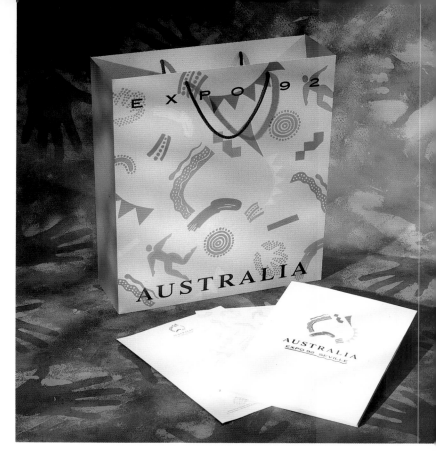

Opposite Page

Wine Label Red Ant Red

Designer David Lancashire

David Lancashire Design

Typographer Godfrey Fawcett

Client David Lancashire Design

**Showbag - Australian Pavilion at Expo
'92 - Seville Designer** FHA Design
Client Department of Arts, Sport,
Environment, Tourism & Territories

Picnic Red Wine Label

Designer Brian Sadgrove

Brian Sadgrove & Associates

Client Hanging Rock Winery

Stationery Products Packaging

Designer Peter Haythornthwaite

Peter Haythornthwaite Design

Photographer Bill Nichol

Client Artifakts Designs

Opposite Page

'Dome' Designer Roland Butcher

Turner Design **Art Director** Neil Turner

Illustrators Roland Butcher, Hilda Chan,

Malcolm Lindsay, Grant Fuller

Typographer Roland Butcher

Client Dome Coffees Australia Limited

Seppelt 100 Year Old Para Liqueur

Designer Barrie Tucker

Barrie Tucker Design Pty Ltd

Art Director Barrie Tucker

Production Manager Sergio Jeloscek

Typographers Elizabeth Schlooz, Barrie

Tucker **Client** B Seppelt & Sons

Gramp's Cabernet Merlot
Designer Barrie Tucker
Barrie Tucker Design Pty Ltd
Art Director Barrie Tucker
Typographers Barrie Tucker, Elizabeth
Schlooz **Client** G Gramp & Sons

Naturalis Toiletries Packaging

Designer Peter Haythornthwaite · Peter Haythornthwaite

Design **Client** Multichem Laboratories

Environmental Graphics

Downing Centre

Designer Emery Vincent Associates

Art Director Garry Emery

Client NSW Public Works Department

Opposite Page

Melbourne

Olympic

Sculptures

Designer

Ken Cato

Cato Design Inc

Client

The Melbourne

Olympic

Candidature 1996

Melbourne Zoo Signage Designer Brier Gough

Melbourne Zoo Graphic Design Section

Photographer Max Delippoulos   **Art Director** Margaret Mason

Illustrators Brier Gough, Tracey Wylie

Typographer Brier Gough   **Client** Healesville Sanctuary

Environmental Graphics

Skydancers-Butterfly Exhibition

Designer Design Studio · Museum of
Victoria **Photographer** Photography
Dept - Museum of Victoria
Client Museum of Victoria

SKYDANCERS

Butterflies of the World

Australia Council Signage

Designer Steven Joseph · Spatchurst

Design Associates **Illustrator** Brett Bush

Client Viv Fraser & Associates

Opposite Page/Above

Laminex Launch Designer Ken Cato

Cato Design Inc **Client** Laminex

Industries

'ADELPHI' Designer Emery Vincent
Associates **Art Director** Garry Emery
Client Denton Corker Marshall Architects

Opposite Page/Above

Tabaret Interior Design Programme Designer Ken Cato

Cato Design Inc **Client** Totalization Board of Australia

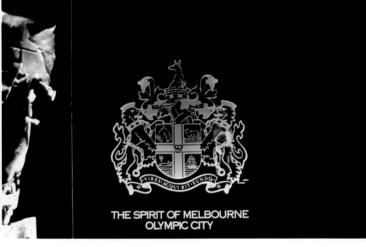

THE SPIRIT OF MELBOURNE
OLYMPIC CITY

Melbourne Olympic Exhibition

Designer Cato Design Inc

Art Director Ken Cato

Client The Melbourne Olympic

Candidature 1996

AROUND AUSTRALIA ●

Australia is the world's oldest land mass formed over 3 billion years ago, featuring some spectacular natural landmarks

Australie est le plus ancien continent, formé il y a plus de 3 milliards d'années. On y trouve des merveilles naturelles très spectaculaires

Opposite Page/Above

Melbourne Zoo Signage

Designer Emery Vincent Associates

Art Director Garry Emery

Client Royal Melbourne Zoological Board

Sandridge Tram

Designer Emery Vincent Associates

Art Director Garry Emery

Client Robert Peck von Hartel

Threthowan Architects

PLEASE DO NOT ENTER

Your journey through the gorilla rainforest will be more interesting and enjoyable if you begin at the entrance near the Main Gate.

GORILLAS

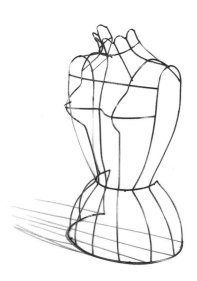

Illustration

Opposite Page

Magazine Article

'The Joy of

Impotence'

Illustrator

Barry Olive

Art Director

Bruce Daly

Client

HQ Magazine

Shopping Bag Illustrators Chris Perks,

Shane Hearn · Cato Design Inc

Designer Chris Perks

Client Rowland Commercial Catering

Self Promotion

Illustrator Kim Roberts-Smith

Kim Roberts-Smith Design & Illustration

Illustration

[212 • 213]

Opposite Page

Review of

Operations

Illustrator

Phil Ritchie

Ritchie Thorburn

Design

Designer

Phil Ritchie

Client

3M Australia

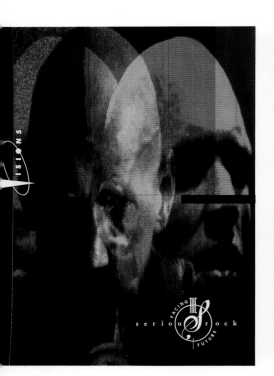 

'Vision' Illustrator Emery Vincent Associates

Art Director Garry Emery **Designer** Emery Vincent Associates

Client Commission for the Future

Illustration

[214•215]

SMOOTH

WETORDRY
RI-M-ITE
PAPER

Self Promotion Illustrator Sarah Wilkins

Designer Sarah Wilkins

'Peace on Earth' Promotional Poster Illustrator Paul Nolan

Nolan Design **Designer** Paul Nolan **Client** Paul Nolan

Household Insurance Article

Illustrator Sue Ninham

Designer Sue Ninham

Art Director Belinda Hempill

Client Good Housekeeping Magazine

Opposite Page

Museum of

Victoria

Exhibition

'You're It'

Illustrator

Julia Church

Client Sunday

Herald Magazine

Illustration

[218 ● 219]

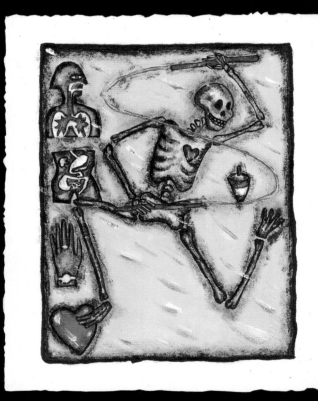

Opposite Page

'Doctor's Dilema'

Illustrator

Nigel Buchanan

Art Director

Tim Donnellan

Client Australian

Penthouse

Magazine

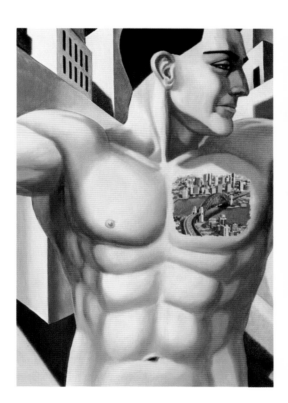 

Metroplaza Book Series Illustrator Michael Golding

Designer Bobbi Gassey **Art Director** Bobbi Gassey

Typographer Bobbi Gassey **Agency** Omon **Client** Industrial

Equities Limited

Illustration

Scraperboard for Gas Co Newspaper Ad

Illustrator Michael Golding

Designer Bobbi Gassey

Art Director Bobbi Gassey

Typographer Bobbi Gassey

Agency Omon **Client** Gas Company

Self Promotion 'Cafe' Illustrator Barry Olive

Poster Illustrator Geoff Kelly

Tou-Can Design Pty Ltd

Designer Warwick Cruise

Client The Paper House

'Tassie Devil'
Illustrator
Geoff Kelly
Tou-Can Design
Pty Ltd
Client Tou-Can
Design Pty Ltd

Illustration

[222*223]

Opposite/Above

Countrylink Banner Illustrations

Illustrator Paul Leith

Designer Sally Richardson

Ginns Design Group Pty Ltd

Art Director Anthony Ginns

Client Countrylink

Self Promotion

'Post Modern'

Illustrator

Michael Golding

Self Promotion Christmas Card Illustrator Davies Davies

Design Pty Ltd **Designer** Davies Davies Design

Opposite Page

Swap Cards

Illustrator

Ned Culic

Ned Culic Design

Art Director

Alex Fenton

Agency J Walter

Thompson

Client Kraft

Illustration

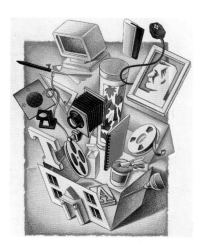

Opposite Page

Book Cover Illustrator Nigel Buchanan

Client Drawing Book Studios

'Exploding House'

Illustrator Ned Culic · Ned Culic Design

Agency Kent & Partners **Client** Showads

Opposite Page

'Legal Liability'

Editorial

Illustration

Illustrator

Sarah Wilkins

Designer

Sarah Wilkins

Client Australian

Accountant

Magazine

'Food for Gifts' Illustrator Ned Culic · Ned Culic Design

Designer Ned Culic **Art Director** Bruce Kneale

Agency HDM Mattingly Advertising **Client** Myer/Grace Bros

Illustration

[228 ● 229]

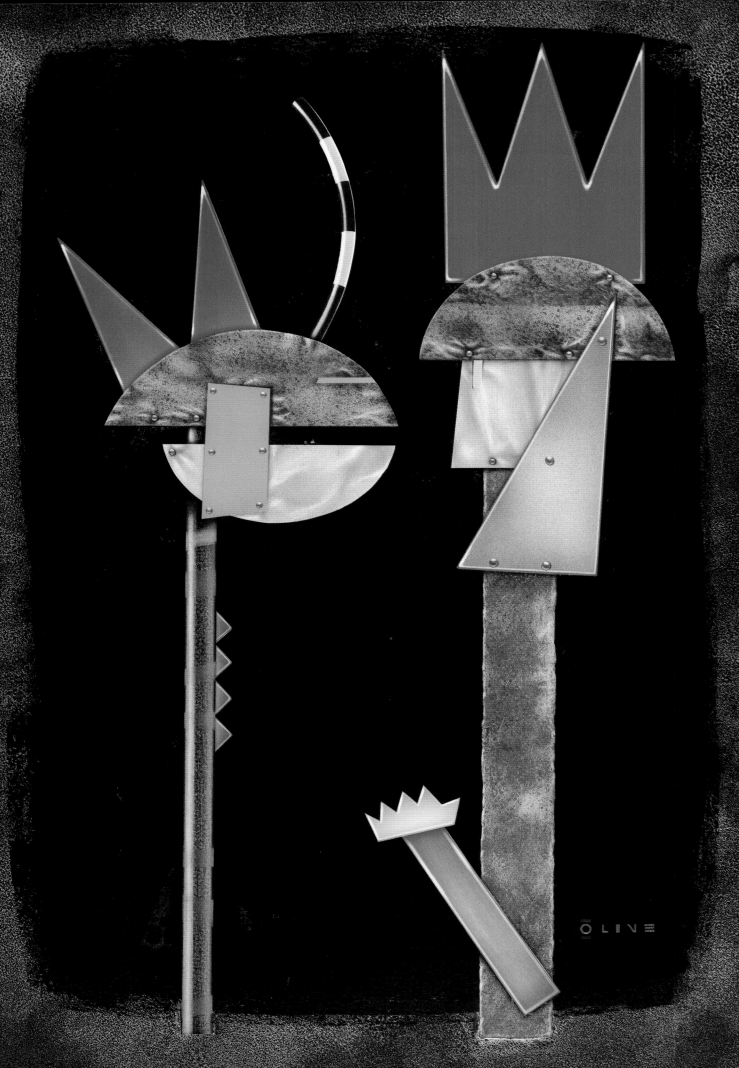

OLINE

Opposite Page

Self Promotion

'Modern

Romance'

Illustrator

Barry Olive

'Haloween' Illustrator Ned Culic · Ned Culic Design

Art Director Maree Coote **Client** Phillip Morris

Christmas Sticker Illustrator Geoff Kelly · Tou-Can Design

Pty Ltd **Designer** Andrew Hook **Client** Cozzolino/Ellett Design

D'Vision

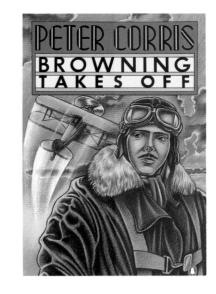

Illustration

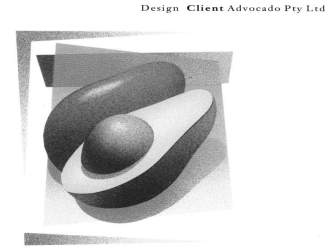

Opposite Page
Magazine Article
**'Women Falling
Down on the
Street'**
Illustrator
Barry Olive
Art Director
Bruce Daly
Client
HQ Magazine

'Romeo & Juliet' Illustrator Julia Church
Client Sunday Herald Magazine

Advocado Identity
Illustrator Nigel Buchanan
Designer Anne Barton · Barton Wendt
Design **Client** Advocado Pty Ltd

Illustration

[234•235]

Photography

Opposite Page/Below

Magazine Article 'Tribal surf dreams'

Photographer Michele Aboud

Michele Aboud Photography

Designer Alyson Bell

Art Director Alyson Bell

Typographer Alyson Bell

Design Group YPMA Publications

Client Interior Architecture

Opposite Page

'Burning Angel'

Self Promotion

Photographer

Ian Hobbs

Adjective

Calendar Photographer Milton Wordley

Milton Wordley & Associates

Designer John Nowland

Art Director John Nowland

Design Group John Nowland Design

Client Petaluma Wines

"LOOKS MORE LIKE A SURFBOARD TO ME."

Chris Strangways,
welder,
Mungeribar, NSW

114

Anodised aluminium and brass "Vertical Smile" lamp by Geoffrey Gifford.

"THE ONLY PROBLEM WITH IT, I SUPPOSE, IS
THAT IT'D TAKE UP A LOT OF ROOM IN MY PLACE."

Kim Turner,
benchman,
Maryola, NSW

115

Self-assembly sassafras (or black bean) and stainless steel
"Grace" clothes stand by Simon Cook for Design Rhetoric.

"IT'D BE OK FOR AN OFFICE OR SOMETHING
LIKE THAT, BUT IT'S A BIT TOO TRENDY FOR ME."

Warren Gleadhill,
crusher operator,
Cobar, NSW

106

Self Promotion Calendar

Photographer Peter Akbiyik

AMPA Productions Pty Ltd

Designer Amanda Roach

Art Director Amanda Roach

Design Group Amanda Roach Design

Opposite Page

'Walter Burley Griffin's Incinerator'

Photographer Bob Baxter

Designer Donna Cavanough

Art Director Alyson Bell

Typographer Donna Cavanough

Design Group YPMA Publications

Client Interior Architecture

'Camels' **Photographer** Richard Gale

Williams Gale **Design Group** JMA - O & M

Client W A Tourism Commission

'Eye Spy' **Photographer** Willem Rethmeier · Willem Rethmeier
Photography **Designer** Alyson Bell **Typographer** Alyson Bell
Client Interior Architecture

Promotional Poster

Photographer Vincent Railton

Fotowerk **Design Group** Fotowerk

Australia **Client** Spicers/Fotowerk

Paper Promotion

Photographer

Lou D'Angelo

Designer

FHA Design

Client Spicers Paper

Calendar 'African Breakfast' Photographer North Sullivan
XYZ (Sydney) **Art Director** Mark Pitt **Agency** O & M Nairobi
(Kenya) **Client** Serena Hotels and Lodges

Brochure 'The Road to Lake Eyre' Photographer North
Sullivan XYZ (Sydney) **Client** Countrylink

'Rough Bark' Bush Furniture

Photographer David Chivers

Ffotograff **Art Director** Alyson Bell

Design Group YPMA Publications

Client Interior Architecture

Aboud, Michele, Photography
8 St Peters Lane
Darlinghurst NSW 2010
Telephone 02 360 1003

Adjective
24/94 Oxford Street
Darlinghurst NSW 2010
Telephone 02 360 3276

AMPA Productions Pty Limited
6 Martin Street
St Kilda Vic 3182
Telephone 03 534 8144

Art of Style, The
300 Bulwara Road
Ultimo NSW 2007
Telephone 02 211 5218

Asprey Di Donato Design
107 Nicholson Street
East Brunswick Vic 3057
Telephone 03 388 0543

Barr, Ross, & Associates Pty Limited
Level 2
2 Glen Street
Milsons Point NSW 2061
Telephone 02 929 0055

Barton Wendt Design
53 Regent Street
Paddington NSW 2021
Telephone 02 360 4307

Baxter, Bob
1/437 Crown Street
Surry Hills NSW 2010
Telephone 02 319 5949

Billy Blue Group, The
The Grandstand
Cnr Miller & Ridge Streets
North Sydney NSW 2065
Telephone 02 957 2844

Bluetree Pty Limited
119 Cathedral Street
Woolloomooloo NSW 2011
Telephone 02 357 7966

Brown, Geoff, Photography
40 Foucart Street
Rozelle NSW 2039
Telephone 02 818 5644

Buchanan, Nigel
243 Riley Street
Surry Hills NSW 2010
Telephone 02 211 1396

C

Callister, Lee, Design
21 Queen Road
Paddington NSW 2021
Telephone 02 331 7902

Cato Design Inc NSW
202 Jersey Road
Woollahra NSW 2025
Telephone 02 327 3866

Cato Design Inc
254 Swan Street
Richmond Vic 3121
Telephone 03 429 6577

Church, Julia
2nd Floor
309-311 Little Collins Street
Melbourne Vic 3000
Telephone 03 654 1511

Cocoon Design Consultancy
8 Eastern Place
Hawthorn East VIC 3123
Telephone 03 882 7860

Corlette Design
2nd floor
360 Pacific Highway
Crows Nest NSW 2065
Telephone 02 439 4922

Cozzolino/Ellett Design D'Vision
8 Eastern Place
Hawthorn East Vic 331223
Telephone 03 882 9711

Crowd Productions Pty Limited
111 Nott Street
Port Melbourne Vic 3207
Telephone 03 646 5727

Culic, Ned, Design
90 Clyde Street
St Kilda Vic 3182
Telephone 03 534 6445

D

Davies Davies Design Pty Limited
4 Goulburn Street
Sydney NSW 2000
Telephone 02 264 8403

Davy, Mary, Design
264 Glenmore Road
Paddington NSW 2021
Telephone 02 360 4422

Debeer Adams Associates
Box 37.594
Parnell
Auckland New Zealand
Telephone 09 366 1253

Denning, Mark, Graphic Design
58A Willoughby Road
Crows Nest NSW 2065
Telephone 02 439 2088

Designworks
PO Box 6335
Wellington New Zealand
Telephone 04 846 164

Done Art and Design
17 Thurlow Street
Redfern NSW 2016
Telephone 02 698 8555

E

Emery Vincent Associates
80 Market Street
South Melbourne Vic 3205
Telephone 03 699 3822

Eymont Kin-Yee Design
8 Soudan Lane
Paddington NSW 2021
Telephone 02 361 5323

F

FHA Design
Level 6
55 Southbank Bld
South Melbourne Vic 3205
Telephone 03 686 9055

Fotowerk
67A Herbert Street
Rosalie Qld 4064
Telephone 07 369 5107

Freeman, Desmond, Associates
Suite 93 Havelock Mall
City West WA 6005
Telephone 09 322 5444

G

Gallaher & Associates
33 Victoria Street
McMahons Point NSW 2060
Telephone 02 957 1655

Gaven, Isabel, Design Pty Limited
5th Floor
24 Bellevue Street
Surry Hills NSW 2010
Telephone 02 211 2074

Ginns Design Group Pty Limited
179 Harris Street
Pyrmont NSW 2009
Telephone 02 552 4388

Golding, Michael
Level 5 24/38 Bellevue Street
Surry Hills NSW 2010
Telephone 02 211 2243

H

Harcus, Annette, Design
30-36 Bay Street
Double Bay NSW 2028
Telephone 02 327 4013

Haythornthwaite, Peter, Design
PO Box 31-263
Milford
Auckland New Zealand
Telephone 09 418 2315

Hero Communications Pty Limited
463 Harris Street
Ultimo NSW 2007
Telephone 02 552 3377

Hulsbosch Pty Limited
24 Young Street
Neutral Bay NSW 2089
Telephone 02 953 0900

Hungerford, Judy, Design Pty Limited
31 Lady Davidson Circuit
Forestville NSW 2087
Telephone 02 451 0810

I

Icarus Industrial Design Pty Limited
62 Weller Street
Goodwood SA 5034
Telephone 08 373 0622

Inhaus Design Pty Limited
76 Aurelia Street
Toongabbie NSW 2146
Telephone 02 631 7100

K

Kajetan Design Group
Suite 21
545 St Kilda Road
Melbourne Vic 3004
Telephone 03 521 1333

Kameruka Design Group
56 Kameruka Road
Northbridge NSW 2063
Telephone 02 958 7105

Kennon, Ian, Advertising
115 Alexander Street
Crows Nest NSW 2065
Telephone 02 439 2611

Kidd, Ian, Design Pty Limited
175 Fullarton Road
Dulwich SA 5065
Telephone 08 332 0000

L

Lam-Po-Tang & Co Pty Limited
38 Ruthven Street
Bondi Junction NSW 2022
Telephone 02 369 1213

Lancashire, David, Design
7 Newry Street
Richmond Vic 3121
Telephone 03 427 1766

Leong, Nelson, Art Direction & Design
Suite 2 · 144 Riley Street
East Sydney NSW 2010
Telephone 02 332 2933

Lewis, Andrew, & Company
223 Pacific Highway
North Sydney NSW 2060
Telephone 02 959 4800

Linear Design Studio
290A Hay Street
Subiaco WA 6008
Telephone 09 382 4311

M

Marsh, Kel, Graphic Design Ltd
111 Richmond Road
Ponsonby
Auckland New Zealand
Telephone 09 788 578

Marshall Arts Graphic Design
92 Clyde Street
St Kilda Vic 3182
Telephone 03 534 7721

Marzi, Michael, Design
15 Bank Street
South Melbourne VIC 3205
Telephone 03 690 0905

Masters, Tony, Design Pty Limited
37 Macdonald Street
Paddington NSW 20221
Telephone 02 332 3122

Mawer, Sue/Boddy, Andrew
Suite 93 Havelock Mall
City West WA 6005
Telephone 09 322 5444

Media Five Australia Pty Limited
PO Box 888
Southport Qld 4215
Telephone 075 32 6055

Melbourne Zoo Graphic Design Section
Elliott Avenue
Parkville Vic 3052
Telephone 03 347 1522

Museum of Victoria
328 Swanston Street
Melbourne Vic 3000
Telephone 03 669 9909

N

Nex Design Group Pty Limited
863 Wellington Street
Perth WA 6000
Telephone 09 322 6118

Ninham, Sue
Level 9
287 Elizabeth Street
Sydney NSW 2000
Telephone 02 264 7744

Nolan Design
PO Box 202
Fortitude Valley Qld 4006
Telephone 07 252 5674

Nowland, John, Design
122 Sturt Street
Adelaide SA 5000
Telephone 08 212 2037

O

Olive, Barry
283 Alfred Street North
North Sydney NSW 2060
Telephone 02 957 5598

O'Reilly, Phil, Design Limited
Level 2
46 Brown Street
Ponsonby
Auckland New Zealand
Telephone 09 788 255

P

Pettigrew, Stuart, Design
Studio 10
545 St. Kilda Road
Melbourne Vic 3004
Telephone 03 529 1037

Phillip Institute of Technology
Design Department
Plenty Road
Bundoora Vic 3083
Telephone 03 468 2285

Powerhouse Museum
659-695 Harris Street
Ultimo NSW 2007
Telephone 02 217 0193

Professional Graphics
605 Darling Street
Balmain NSW 2042
Telephone 02 818 4044

R

Rankin Bevers Design
502 Albert Street
East Melbourne Vic 3002
Telephone 03 666 1233

Reno Visual Communications
PO Box 50
Broadway NSW 2007
Telephone 02 698 4388

Rethmeier, Willem, Photography
4th Floor · 134 Broadway
Sydney NSW 2007
Telephone 02 281 1558

Ritchie Thorburn Design
5/407 Glebe Point Road
Glebe NSW 2037
Telephone 02 692 0566

Robert-Smith, Kim, Design & Illustration
60A Pleasant Road
East Hawthorn Vic 3123
Telephone 03 882 6206

Roffey, David, Design
74 Chisholm Avenue
Clareville NSW 2107
Telephone 02 918 3067

S

Sadgrove, Brian, & Associates
6 Little Page Street
Albert Park Vic 3206
Telephone 03 690 8977

Shepherd, Robert
Suite 1 · 21-25 Rowe Street
Eastwood NSW 2122
Telephone 02 858 1988

Siren
30 Wilson Street
Newtown NSW 2042
Telephone 02 550 4811

Spatchurst Design Associates
157 Brougham Street
Kings Cross NSW 2011
Telephone 02 358 5866

Springham Design
39 Hay Street
Subiaco WA 6008
Telephone 09 382 3133

Stumfel, Andrew
105 Brandon Street
Kensington WA 6151
Telephone 09 474 1359

Swinburne Design Group
PO Box 218
Hawthorn Vic 3122
Telephone 03 819 8143

T

TCG Graphic Design
53 Balfour Street
Chippendale NSW 2008
Telephone 02 699 8300

TKR Graphics
104-106 Wigram Street
Parramatta NSW 2150
Telephone 02 633 4188

Tou-Can Design Pty Limited
13 Old Heidelberg Road
Alphington Vic 3078
Telephone 03 499 3169

Tucker, Barrie, Design Pty Limited
245 Fullarton Road
Eastwood SA 5063
Telephone 08 373 0616

Turner Design
1st floor
61 King Street
Perth WA 6000
Telephone 09 321 3811

U

Ultragraphics
290A Hay Street
Subiaco WA 6008
Telephone 09 382 2297

V

Veal, Dennis, Design
GPO Box 598
Brisbane Qld 4001
Telephone 07 221 3920

W

Wilkins, Sarah
8 Eastern Place
Hawthorn East Vic 3123
Telephone 03 882 0024

Williams Gale
1 Price Street
Jolimont WA 6014
Telephone 09 388 2144

Wood Pratt Wallace Design
169 Dowling Street
Woolloomooloo NSW 2011
Telephone 02 358 5777

Wordley, Milton, & Associates
25 Selby Street
Adelaide SA 5000
Telephone 08 231 0155

X

XYZ (Sydney)
56 Sophia Street
Surry Hills NSW 2010
Telephone 02 212 5799

Y

YPMA Publications
2nd Floor
54 Oxford Street
Darlinghurst NSW 2010
Telephone 02 332 4560

A book such as "Design Down Under"
comes together only through the efforts
of many people.
Particular contributions deserve
recognition.

Book Design

Ginns Design Group Pty. Ltd.

Design Direction

Anthony Ginns · Pia Smeaton ·
Philipp Geisert

Artwork

Pagemakers

Forewords

Olaf Leu · Massimo Vignelli ·
Henry Steiner

Publication Co-ordination

Beverley Middleton · Marina Dixon

Organisation

Raymond Bennett · Ned Culic

Contributors

Canberra Press · Show Ads · Ian Freeman
Paragraph The Type Studio · Tandy
Rowley · Edwards Dunlop & B.J. Ball ·
Bibelot

Printing

Toppan Printing Co. Limited

Acknowledgements

DESIGN DOWN UNDER 2

Design Down Under
2/29 Berry Street
North Sydney NSW 2060
Australia
Telephone 02 923 2641
Facsimile 02 923 2496

ISBN 0.646 05636.0
ISSN 1033.4467

Editor
Jennifer Overend Prior, Ph.D.

Managing Editor
Ina Massler Levin, M.A.

Editor-in-Chief
Sharon Coan, M.S. Ed.

Illustrator
Renée Christine Yates

Cover Artist
Lesley Palmer

Art Coordinator
Kevin Barnes

Art Director
CJae Froshay

Imaging
Temo Parra
Rosa C. See

Product Manager
Phil Garcia

Publishers
Rachelle Cracchiolo, M.S. Ed.
Mary Dupuy Smith, M.S. Ed.

A Year of Themes
Science & Social Studies
GRADES 1-2

Author

Sarah Kartchner Clark, M.A.

Teacher Created Materials, Inc.
6421 Industry Way
Westminster, CA 92683
www.teachercreated.com
ISBN-0-7439-3715-5
©2004 Teacher Created Materials, Inc.
Made in U.S.A.

S0-DUT-034

Table of Contents

Introduction

With all the demands of our world, literacy is becoming increasingly vital. Though "literacy" is an often-used word in education today, many children in the world are growing up without a strong literacy foundation. Just what is literacy? The dictionary states that a literate person is one who is able to read and write.

The purpose of *A Year of Themes: Social Studies and Science* is to provide a literacy-rich environment in which children learn to use and enjoy written and spoken language and see the connections to social studies and science. The children will become immersed in print and use their developing language and social studies/science skills in purposeful activities. Students will learn phonetic sounds, hear rhyme and rhythm, and begin to understand language structure and scientific concepts. *A Year of Themes: Social Studies and Science* uses short stories and rhymes to set a comfortable tone for the students.

This book is divided into nine units—one for each month of the traditional school year. Each segment is based on a theme and has a literature selection and math activities. Each segment in this book is organized to include some or all of the following activities:

- lesson plans
- related literature suggestions
- guest speaker suggestions
- learning centers
- scientific activities/demonstrations
- journal writing ideas
- exposure to nonfiction text

- reproducible little books
- science/social studies games
- group discussion
- art projects
- story-related visual aids
- drama activities
- scientific experiments

Social Studies/Science Standards and Objectives

All educators should be accountable for teaching skills and objectives that will promote social studies, science, and literacy. Listed below are the objectives and skills that are taught in this book.

Social Studies

- Recognize school rules and their importance
- Identify traits and characteristics that make each of us unique
- Identify friendship traits (i.e., honesty, kindness, cooperation, etc.)
- Identify and locate holidays on a calendar
- Describe the jobs that people do in the community

Science

- Identify the five senses and what they do
- Identify basic earth materials
- Perform simple comparisons and experiments
- Identify how the weather affects daily activities

A Year of Themes in Social Studies and Science

This book is divided into nine sections providing you with a different theme and literature selection for each month of the traditional school year. Use the themes to teach skills and information and use the literature selections to teach literacy, social studies, and science concepts. Here is a suggested outline:

September—Our Classroom

Start the school year off by focusing on your class and the rules and guidelines that will help your students to be successful. The little book "Going to School" will discuss starting the school year off right, with a focus on community/classroom skills and rules.

October—Me, Myself, and I

Each of us is unique and has our own talents and abilities. Help your students discover their individual worth. "I Like Me!" discusses the unique traits and characteristics we all have. Build self-esteem as your students learn about themselves.

November—Friends

Everybody needs a friend. Sometimes children lack the skills to make friends. This unit focuses on friendship and how it is developed. The little book "Friendship" discusses many different ways your students can make and keep friends. Use this unit to identify friendship traits.

December—Holidays Are Here!

What is life without the holidays? Explore the different holidays that your students celebrate. Do not hesitate to add holidays to study that might not be mentioned in this unit. Expose your students to holidays celebrated throughout the world. Teach them how to mark and identify holidays on the calendar.

January—People in Our Community

Learning about the people in the community not only helps students understand the world they live in, but it can also make it a friendlier place to be. Invite guest speakers to come in and discuss their jobs with students. Encourage students to think about what they want to be when they grow up. Use this unit to describe jobs that people have in the community.

February—My Senses

This science unit explores the senses and how they work. This active unit gives hands-on experience with the five senses. The little book "My Senses" teaches the purpose of each of the senses. Students will love the activities they do with their eyes, ears, hands, nose, and mouth to explore their world.

March—Rocks, Rocks, Rocks

Everybody needs a rock! This unit will help students identify basic earth materials. The most basic of these is the rock. There are many things you can do with a rock. Read the little book "My Rock Book" to see what options are available.

April—Seeds and Plants

Have you ever planted a garden? The planting and growing of a seed is a miracle. Introduce your students to the miracle of seeds and plants. Use this unit to perform simple comparisons and experiments. Your "budding" scientists will love to see their plants grow.

May—Weather

The little book, "My Book of Weather" lends itself easily to learning about weather. This unit will help students identify how weather affects their daily activities. Grab your coats!

Preparing this Social Studies/Science Literacy Unit

There is no stop and start to literacy. Encouraging literacy can be a continuous process filling every waking minute. Immersing your students in literacy and math activities can build a solid foundation for years to come. Listed below are activities and suggestions you can implement to make *A Year of Themes: Science and Social Studies* a success in your classroom.

Making the Little Books

There are nine well-known stories and poems used to teach literacy in this book. Each story or poem comes with little books for your students. Reproduce the pages of the little books. Books may be assembled before the lesson or students may help complete the following steps. 1. Cut on the lines. 2. Check to make sure the pages are in the correct order. 3. Then staple the pages together. Students may use crayons or colored pencils to color their little books. Be sure to allow time for students to read them independently, with partners, or as a class. When you have finished studying the books in class, send them home for students to share with their families.

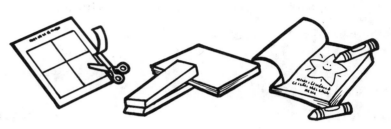

Activity Pages

There are activity pages to go with each little book. These activity pages are used to give students practice in reading, writing, and solving problems. Reproduce the activity pages for the students as needed. Directions for using the activity pages are provided in the lesson plans. You will find pages introducing the social studies or science focus for that unit.

Literacy Journals

Reading the stories and poems in this book can provide many opportunities for students to reflect on their own life experiences. Set aside time for students to "write" and record in their journals. They can express their thoughts and ideas through pictures and words. Write a question on the chalkboard for students to respond to in their journals. Make a literacy journal simply by stapling lined sheets of paper inside two sheets of construction paper. Encourage students to design pictures for the covers. Once students have responded to the questions in their journals, be sure to allow time for them to share what they have written and drawn.

Word Wall

Set aside a place in your classroom to write down easy-to-read, common words that are found in the little books. Allow students to practice reading these words before, during, and after they read the little books. Encourage students to add words they think need to be added to the word wall. Add social studies and science words to your word wall as you come across them in your studies.

On the Lookout

Encourage students to look for information related to the topics being studied. Students may find newspaper articles, magazine articles, letters, books, stories, etc. Bring in any kind of information that appropriately teaches and addresses the themes taught. Share and discuss these as a class, and post them for future reference.

Going to School

It's time for school,
It's time for fun.
And there is room
For everyone!

Stories we'll write
Books to be read
Pictures we'll draw
And songs, Teacher said.

So join the class
Be safe, be kind.
We'll follow the rules,
We'll learn, we'll mind.

6

Going to School Lesson Plans

Week One

1. Gather students in a circle and have a class discussion about starting school. What feelings are students feeling? What activities and projects will they be excited to know about? What other information will be helpful to them? What procedures do you want your students to know? This first class meeting can soothe concerns and worries. You may end the class discussion by reading one of the books about the beginning of school. (See the bibliography on page 96.) Hold up the little book "Going to School." Explain to students that you are going to read a poem about starting school.

2. Read the poem "Going to School." You may copy and enlarge page 6 to use for this activity. Be sure to read the poem two or three times. As you read the poem aloud, encourage your students to join in when they can. Point to each word in the poem as you read it.

3. Discuss with students why rules are important in a classroom. What would happen if there weren't any rules? Have students brainstorm rules that might be helpful in your classroom. List each of the rules on the chalkboard. Combine the rules that are similar and add any rules that you see may be lacking. Discuss each rule with your class members. Does everyone agree that these are the rules for this class? Have students act out each rule. You might also want to use the rules listed on page 12. Adopt this page of rules or use this page to guide and direct the writing of your own class rules. Copy your class rules onto a large sheet of posterboard. Leave room below the rules at the bottom of the poster. Read the final rules carefully. After the rules have been determined, have each student sign his or her name at the bottom of the poster signifying that each student promises to try to follow the class rules. Display this poster in a prominent location in your classroom.

4. Distribute copies of the little books for "Going to School." Have students color the pages of this book and then cut them out. Help students assemble and staple their books together. Pair students with partners and have them read their little books together.

Week Two

1. The focus for this little book is recognizing school rules and their importance. Brainstorm with students what might happen if there weren't any school rules.

2. Distribute copies of page 13. Assign a specific class rule to each student. Using the space in the apple, each student illustrates the rule he or she has been assigned. Be sure to have crayons or markers and scissors available for students to use. When they have finished illustrating their apple shapes, have students cut them out. You may choose to have students share their illustrations in small groups or as a class. Post these apple shapes on a bulletin board in your class.

Going to School Lesson Plans *(cont.)*

Week Three

1. Explain to students that following classroom rules is important. It is important for students to know the classroom routines in order for them to be successful. What expectations do you have for them? What do you want your students to do when they first come into the classroom? What are the procedures for getting ready for a snack or time to go home? Where should students put finished work? What can they do if they finish their work early? Answering these questions ahead of time will eliminate some behavior problems. Practice routines with students. Point out tips that will help them remember these routines. Review these procedures and routines frequently at the beginning and be sure to model appropriate behavior. Don't forget to reteach these procedures as the need arises.

2. Read "Going to School" to the students. Next, read a different story about starting school or following the rules in the classroom. (See the bibliography on page 96.) Discuss the similarities and differences between the stories. If time allows, discuss the school rules that were either followed or ignored in the story.

3. Write the lines of the poem on different sentence strips. Post the sentence strips out of order on the chalkboard. Have students assist you in placing the strips in order. Read the sentences again to check the sequence. Make changes as needed.

4. Read the poem again with the students while they follow along in their little books. Point to each word as you read it, but allow students to do more and more of the reading on their own.

5. Getting to know each other can also help students start to feel comfortable in the classroom. Gather your students in a circle. Have students roll a ball to each other. As students catch the rolling ball, have them say their names. After all students have been able to share their names at least once or twice, see how many names your students can remember. Instead of saying their own names, have students "catch" the rolling ball and then say the name of the person they are rolling the ball to next. If a child says the correct name, play continues in the same manner. If the student says the wrong name, the student is corrected and then play continues. Be sure to join in with your class so you can learn names and the students get to know you as well!

Week Four

1. Divide your class into small groups. With adult supervision, go on a scavenger hunt (see page 14) looking for important items in the classroom or around the school. Are there important places or people to introduce to the students? For example, the principal, the school nurse, the secretaries in the office, etc.? Do students know where to enter and exit the school? Do they know where the playground is? Have them share their findings with each other when they return to class.

2. At the end of this mini unit, have a class meeting to allow students a chance to discuss their feelings about the new school year and the classroom. Are there new concerns that need to be addressed? Use page 15 to help in your discussion. This page has scenarios of things that might happen. Brainstorm solutions as a class.

Social Studies Literacy in the Works

This page provides learning center suggestions that can be used to reinforce skills taught and discussed in the classroom. Select the centers that you think would best meet the needs of your students.

Math Center

- Provide clipboards, paper, and pencils for students to tally up the number of things they can find in the classroom. How many desks are there? How many chairs are there? How many students are there? How many teachers are there? How many pencils are there? Have students draw pictures of things they find in the classroom and write tally marks beside the corresponding picture.

Reading Center

- Set up an area in your room (complete with large bean bags, pillows, and chairs) for independent reading. Keep a shelf of books available at all times for students to read and browse. For this center, have books available for students about starting school and learning in a classroom. (See bibliography on page 96.)

- Provide sentence strips containing the lines from the poem. At this center, have students work together to read the sentences and determine the correct sequence. Have a little book of the poem available for students to check their work.

Writing Center

- Allow time for students to write in their literacy journals. Be sure to have a literacy journal available for each student with his or her name on it. (See page 5 for directions.) Provide topics for students to write about or leave it up to them to decide. Encourage students to write or draw pictures about their experiences at school. What are they learning? What concerns do they have? Who are their classmates? What do they like most about school?

- Assign each student a letter of the alphabet. At this center, each student will illustrate a picture of something in the classroom that begins with the letter he or she has been assigned. At the end, put all of the pages in order and bind them to make a class book. Share this book with the class and acknowledge each student for his or her contribution.

Art Center

- Set up an easel with paper. Have students use watercolor paints to paint pictures of their classroom. Also, have the "Going to School" poem displayed as a poster, so the students can paint the different phrases in the poem. Display the illustrations around the room when the paintings are dry. Have students sequence the illustrations, placing them in order.

Dramatic Play Center

- Set up a mini-classroom inside your classroom. Students will enjoy writing on a whiteboard and "reading" from books. Use stuffed animals as the pretend students. Provide clipboards, books, pencils, crayons, paper, and other items for this pretend classroom. Be sure that each student gets a turn to be teacher.

Making the Little Book

Going
to
School

1

It's time for school, it's time for fun! **2**

And there is room for everyone! **3**

Stories we'll write! **4**

Making the Little Book *(cont.)*

Books to be read!   5

Pictures we'll draw! and songs, Teacher said.   6

So join the class, be safe, be kind.   7

We'll follow the rules, we'll learn, we'll mind.   8

Our Classroom Rules

Classroom Rules

1. Enter the classroom quietly and take your seat.

2. Keep hands and feet to yourself.

3. Follow teacher directions.

4. Keep your work area clean.

5. Do your best work.

Rules for Good Listening

1. Eyes are watching.

2. Ears are listening.

3. Hands are still.

4. Feet are resting.

5. Mouths are quiet.

School Rules Bulletin Board

Classroom Scavenger Hunt

Can you find these things in your classroom? Write yes or no to record your findings.

Classroom Items	Yes	No
Books		
Pencil sharpener		
Sink		
Clock		
Classroom pet		
Windows		
Teacher		
Ruler		
Crayons		
Paper		
Desks		
Pencils		
Rocking chair		
Door		
Chairs		

What other things are in your classroom? Draw pictures of them below.

14

Scenarios

It's always good to review procedures and rules in your classroom. Giving your students a chance to discuss and anticipate what they can do in a given situation can elevate their level of success in your classroom. During a class discussion, review these scenarios with your class. Be sure to allow students to share their views and address all concerns.

1. You have just gone outside on the playground to play. You decide to go on the swings. You have the swing in one hand when another student comes up and holds the other end of the swing. You both want to ride on the swing. What should you do?

2. It is time to line up to go home. Where do you line up? How should you line up? What should you be doing while you are standing in line?

3. Your teacher is telling you a story about a dog. You can't hear the story. What should you do?

4. Your teacher just asked you to work with a certain person in your class. You really wanted to work with someone else. You really don't want to work with this student. What should you do?

5. You are really thirsty. You need a drink of water. What should you do? Where do you get a drink? How do you get a drink?

6. The bell rings and you are walking into the classroom. What should you do? Where does your backpack go? What else do you need to do to be ready for the day?

7. You are sharing crayons with another classmate. You need the brown crayon to color your tree trunk, but the other student is using it. What can you do? What should you remember?

8. Your teacher gives directions about an assignment. You don't understand what to do. Everyone else is getting to work, but you still don't know what you are supposed to do. What should you do?

9. You were asked to take the attendance to the office. On the way to the office, you get lost and you don't know where to go. What should you do?

10. The teacher blows a whistle and asks you to come in from recess. What are you supposed to do when you hear the whistle? What should you do with your feet, mouth, and hands while you are in line?

11. You are playing on the playground and you see another child get hurt. The teacher doesn't know that this child is hurt. What should you do?

I Like Me!

There's no one else like me,
And that's just how it goes.

From all the way up top,
Right down to wiggly toes!

I like some things about me,
But there are things I don't.

They still are all a part of me,
So change myself? I won't.

I like to sing my songs,
I like to laugh and play.

I'm glad that I am me,
And that is what I say!

16

I Like Me! Lesson Plans

Week One

1. To begin this lesson, provide a mirror for students to use. This can be a full-length mirror or several smaller hand mirrors. Ask students to tell you what they see. Who is this person? How would he or she describe the person in the mirror? What does he or she like about this person? Is there anyone in the classroom that looks exactly the same? Why not? Then distribute crayons and copies of page 22 and ask them to draw pictures of themselves. What color is their hair? What color are their eyes? What other unique features need to be included? Have students share their illustrations. See if students can guess which student is being portrayed. Discuss how different and unique we are. Write the name of each student on the illustration. Make a class book of these unique people in your class. (Be sure to add your own personal illustration as well.)

2. Play a guessing game with students. Begin by describing a student without looking directly at him or her. Describe colors and clothes this student is wearing. What color is his or her hair? What color are his or her eyes? Continue adding descriptions until a student can guess who is being described. Next, select a student to describe another student. Explain how we each have features that make us unique.

3. Explain to the students that you are going to read a poem. This poem is about how we are all different from each other, but that each of us is an important person. Make a large chart of the poem on page 16. Read the poem aloud.

4. Distribute copies of the little books "I Like Me!" Have students color the pages of this book and then cut them out. Help students assemble and staple their books together. Pair students with partners and have them read their little books together.

Week Two

1. The focus for this little book is identifying characteristics that make each of us unique. Read "I Like Me!" aloud. Have students follow along in their little books. Point to each word as you read it. After reading the story, have students look for words. Write the word *me* on the chalkboard and ask students to find and point to the word. Other words to look for are *like*, *head*, *toes*, *don't*, *won't*, *songs*, *smile*, and *play*.

2. To show the differences between two individuals, complete a Venn diagram to compare two students. Draw two large circles that intersect on the chalkboard. In the left circle, ask students to list descriptions of the first student. What words describe how this student looks, acts, and thinks? What talents does this student have? Class members can ask questions of the student as needed. Now on the right circle, do the same with the other student. Where the circles intersect, write the things that are the same about these two students. Are they both wearing jeans? Are they both girls? Do they both like soccer? Do they both have brown hair? Discuss the similarities between the two students. Now distribute copies of the Venn diagram on page 23 and have pairs of students analyze and compare similarities and differences.

I Like Me! Lesson Plans *(cont.)*

Week Three

1. Make a silhouette of each of your students. This can be done by posting a sheet of black construction paper to the wall. Use a lamp or an overhead projector to shine a light on the student as he or she stands in front of the construction paper. A shadow of the student should show up on the black paper. Adjust the size of the shadow by bringing the light source closer or farther away from the student. Trace the shadow of the student on the black paper with a pencil. Then cut out the silhouette.

2. Read stories to your students about other children their age (see Bibliography on page 96.) Then, have a discussion about the similarities and differences between the students and the characters in the stories.

3. Read "I Like Me!" again with the students while they follow along in their little books. Point to each word as you read it, but allow students to do more and more of the reading on their own.

4. Gather students together and have a class discussion about favorite memories. Ask them to share favorite memories of birthdays, holidays, summers, school, vacations, or family events. Encourage each of the students to share at least one memory. Discuss how the memories are similar and different. Distribute copies of the memory book cover on page 24.

5. Have students illustrate pictures for their covers. Insert sheets of paper for students to illustrate different memories. Bind the memory books together and allow students to share their favorite memories with the class.

Week Four

1. Explain to the students that we each have likes and dislikes. These likes and dislikes make us unique. On the chalkboard write, *My favorite food is . . . .* Then have each student copy these words and add an ending to the sentence. Remind each student to put a period at the end of the sentence. Provide crayons or colored pencils and have students illustrate their sentences. Have a sharing time for students to share their sentences.

2. It is important for your students to know their first and last names, their phone numbers, and their home addresses. Spend time in class reviewing these with your students and encourage parents to work at home with their children. Use page 25 to create name/address/phone number cards. Write the information and then have students trace over your writing. Quiz your students to determine whether they have learned this important information.

3. To reinforce the similarities and differences among the children in your classroom, play the "Marching Me" game. Gather your students in a circle and play marching music in the background. Now, randomly call out different facts and characteristics. If the fact matches a child, he or she is to stand up and march around the circle and return to his or her seat. Facts may include things such as, "I like pizza." "I have brown hair." "I am the oldest in my family." "I like vegetables." "I am a girl." "I have a *b* in my name".

Social Studies Literacy in the Works

This page provides learning center suggestions that can be used to reinforce skills taught and discussed in the classroom. Select the centers that you think would best meet the needs of your students.

Listening Center

- Make an audio tape of the "I Like Me!" poem and have students listen to it using a cassette player with headphones. Provide other tape-recorded stories that tell about children the same age as your students.

Dramatic Play Center

- Provide clothes, shoes, hats, ties, and other clothing items for students to try on and explore. Be sure to have a full-length mirror available for students to view themselves.

Reading Center

- Have a variety of books available for students to look at and read. Ask students to identify similarities and differences between themselves and the characters in the books.

Art Center

- Supply students with dough or clay to make figures of themselves. What color are their pants? What color are their shirts? Have students add hair and other features to create replicas of themselves.

- Have students browse through discarded magazines looking for pictures that portray the interests and likes of the students. Have each student cut these pictures from magazines and paste them onto a sheet of construction paper to make a "ME" collage. Display the collages around your classroom for decoration.

Writing Center

- Supply paper, crayons, and other materials needed for students to write poems about themselves. Students may draw pictures in place of words if necessary. Post the chart of the "I Like Me!" poem at this center. Students may use the "I Like Me!" poem as a guide or they may create a new format.

Science Center

- Have pictures of people available for students to observe. At this center, students are to identify similarities and differences between the different people. Have students sort and categorize the pictures into different piles. Extend this center by cutting out pictures of baby animals and their parents. Mount these pictures on index cards. Have students match the animals together. Have students determine the differences between adults and babies.

Math Center

- Write a different number on each of several sheets of paper and distribute them to students at this center. Then, using old magazines have students cut out pictures of things they like. The number of pictures cut out and pasted should match the number on the paper. Have students compare their pictures with other students. Did they end up cutting out the same pictures?

Making the Little Book

I
Like
Me

1

There's no one else like me, and that's just how it goes.   2

From all the way up top, right down to wiggly toes!   3

I like some things about me, but there are things I don't.   4

Making the Little Book *(cont.)*

They still are all a part of me, so change myself? I won't. 5

I like to sing my songs, I like to laugh and play. 6

I'm glad that I am me, and that is what I say! 7

The End 8

My Self Portrait

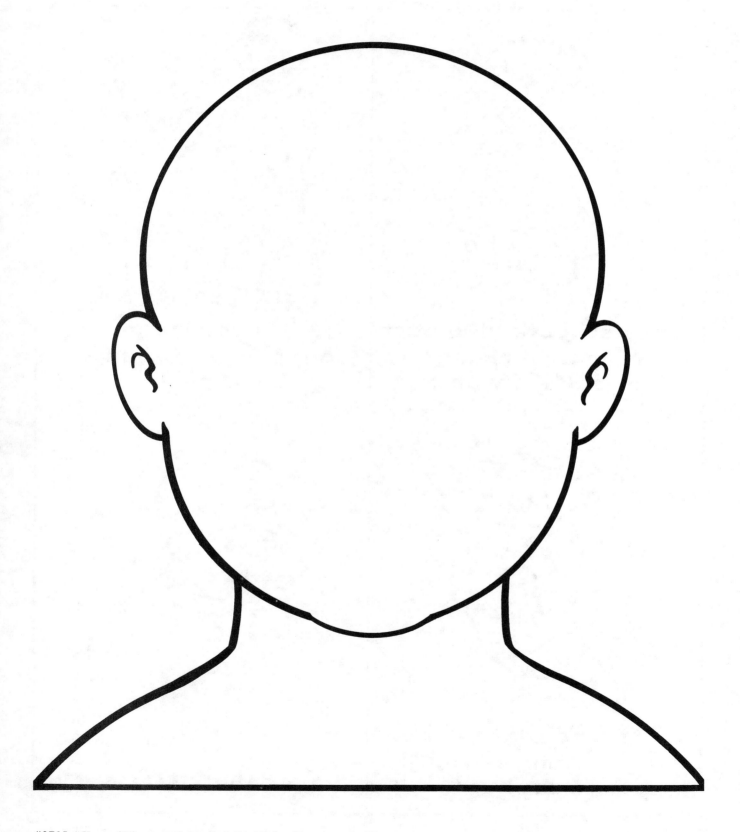

Comparing You and Me!

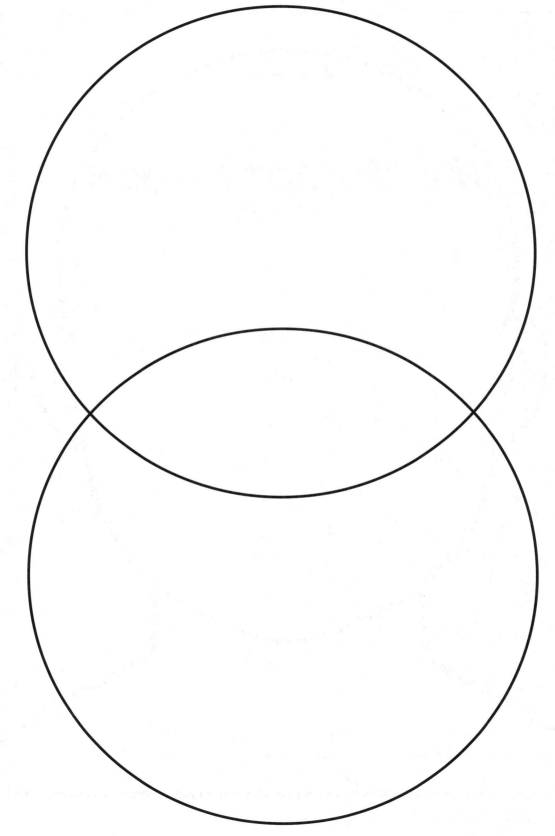

My Memory Book

My Personal Information

Write your personal information inside each box below. Cut each box out and staple them together. Practice reading and recognizing your name, phone number, and address.

My Name

_____

- -

_____

My Phone Number

_____

- -

_____

My address

_____

- -

_____

- -

_____

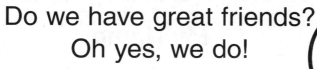

Friendship

Do we have great friends?
Oh yes, we do!

We're singing some songs,
We're reading, too!

Counting and sharing
Can make our day.

Talking and caring,
And time for play!

Running or jumping
Can make us smile!

Laughing and learning
All the while.

Helping our friends
Is what we do.

It is the way,
Our hearts are true.

We have great friends,
Oh yes, we do!

Friendship Lesson Plans

Week One

1. Ask students to think about their friends. Who are they? Why are they friends? What do students like to do with their friends? Discuss as a class why friends are important. Explain to your class that you will read a poem about friendship. Encourage them to listen for things that make good friends.

2. Copy page 26 on chart paper. Display this poster for students to see as you read the poem aloud to your students. Read the poem again and ask them to locate words that describe what good friends are like. Next, ask students to look for descriptions of things mentioned in the poem that they can do with their friends.

3. Distribute copies of the little books of "Friendship." Have students color the pages of their books and then cut them out. Help students assemble and staple their books together. Pair students with partners and have them read their little books together.

4. Working together on a project can build and strengthen friendships. Plan to make the Friendship Fruit Salad (page 32) as a class. Be sure to have extra parental help on this day. Plan ahead to make sure ingredients are sent in to the classroom.

Week Two

1. The focus for this little book is identifying friendship traits. Brainstorm as a class a list of friendship traits. These traits might include being caring, patient, respectful, kind, sharing, happy, inviting, a good listener, etc. You will want to have a discussion of what these words mean. Discuss with your students how you can be a good friend. What does it take to be a good friend?

2. Read "Friendship" aloud to students. Have students follow along in their little books. Model how to point to each word as you read it. After reading the story, have students look for words. Write the word friends on the chalkboard and ask students to find and point to the word in their little books. Other words to look for are *songs*, *count*, *read*, *need*, *share*, *care*, *run*, *jump*, *laugh*, *play*, *talk*, and *listen*. Discuss how illustrations and pictures can help students locate words. Have students complete page 33, matching the actions with the friendship traits.

3. Write a story about friendship as a class. Begin the story yourself by introducing a character in need of a friend. Hold a beanbag as you tell the story. After the story is started, pass the beanbag to a student. The student picks up the story where you left off and adds to it. When this student has shared as little or as much as he or she desires, the student passes the beanbag to another student in the circle. When the story is finished, write each student's contribution to the story on a sheet of paper. Have the student make an illustration to go with the words on this page. Compile these pages together to make a book. Read the book together and keep this book in the class library so students can read it often.

Friendship Lesson Plans *(cont.)*

Week Three

1. Discuss things that can be done with friends. Have each student act out charades of things that can be done with friends. Let the rest of the class guess what the student is acting out.

2. Read the little book to the students. Now read another story about friends. (See the Bibliography on page 96.) Discuss the similarities and differences between the two stories about friendships. Ask students if these stories are real or make-believe. Read other stories you can find about friends. Discuss whether these stories are real or make-believe.

3. Read the story again with the students while they follow along in their little books. Point to each word as you read it, but allow students to do more and more of the reading on their own.

4. Before class, make a list of questions about friendship and write them on strips of paper. Place these strips in a bowl. Invite each student to select a strip of paper from the bowl. Help each student read the question about friendship. Then, have the student answer the question. He or she can ask classmates for help if needed. Also, have students write questions to be answered by the class.

Week Four

1. Explain to the students that friends are important. We need to learn how to be good friends. Have each student think of a special friend that he or she would like to thank. When the student has a friend in mind, have him or her use the letter outline on page 34 to write a letter to this friend.

2. Write the names of all your students on slips of paper. Put all names in a bowl and let each student select a name. Each student then writes a friendship award to give to this student. Distribute copies of page 35 to your students to help make their awards. Conduct a Friends Award Assembly and let students give each other their awards.

3. Play Buddy Tag with your class. This game is played like regular tag except that each student holds hands with a classmate. If one friend is tagged then both students must freeze.

Social Studies Literacy in the Works

This page provides learning center suggestions that can be used to reinforce skills taught and discussed in the classroom. Select the centers that you think would best meet the needs of your students.

Math Center

- For this center, supply students with sheets of paper and crayons. Students then draw pictures of all their friends and/or family members. When students have finished drawing their friends, have them count their friends. Students should then write this number on their paper.

Reading Center

- Write the lines of the friendship poem on different sentence strips. At this center, have students work together to read the sentences and figure out the sequence of the poem. Which strip comes first? Which one comes next? Have a little book of this poem available for students to check their work.

- Set up an area in your room for independent reading. Provide beanbags, pillows, or chairs for more comfort. Keep a bookshelf of books available at all times for students to read and browse. For this center, provide books about friends. These can be stories about friends or they can be nonfiction books about developing friendship traits.

Art Center

- Help students learn to make paper dolls. Fold a sheet of paper into fourths. On the top of the folded paper, trace the design of a body. Be sure that one of the hands is placed on the fold of the paper so two dolls will be connected at the hands once they are cut out.

- Cut along the lines for the other areas of the doll. Once cut, each student will have two dolls connected at the hands. Have each student decorate one of the dolls to be himself or herself and then the other one to be a special friend. Schedule a time for students to share their paper dolls and tell about their friends. These little friend dolls can be used as a border on a bulletin board or can be sent home with the students.

Writing Center

- Have students write in their literacy journals. (See page 5 for directions.) Assign a specific question for students to respond to in their journals or leave it open and let students write about their friends.

Dramatic Play Center

- Provide a flannel board and flannel board pictures of people for students at this center. Have students act out friendship experiences with the flannelboard figures. Also, have students act out friendship problems with these figures and work to get them resolved. Be sure to have plenty of figures available so that each child can play independently of other students.

Making the Little Book

Do We Have Great Friends?

1

Oh yes, we do!
We're singing
some songs,
We're reading, too! 2

Counting and sharing
can make our day. 3

Talking and caring,
and time for play! 4

Making the Little Book *(cont.)*

Running or jumping can make us smile! 5

Laughing and learning all the while. 6

Helping our friends is what we do. 7

It is the way, our hearts are true. We have great friends, oh yes, we do! 8

Friendship Recipe

Make the friendship recipe below with your class. Use the parent letter at the bottom of the page to organize this activity by checking the item you would like the student to bring.

Friendship Fruit Salad

- 2 apples, peeled, cored, and diced
- 2 bananas, sliced
- 2 cans pineapple chunks
- 1 cup watermelon, seeded and cut into small pieces
- 1 cup cantaloupe, seeded and cut into small pieces
- 1 cup miniature marshmallows
- Combine all of the fruit and marshmallows into a large bowl. Serve.

A fruit dressing can be made by mixing 8 ounces of whipped topping and one 8-ounce carton of fruit yogurt together. Add a dollop of the fruit dressing to each serving of Friendship Fruit Salad.

Note: check for food allergies.

Dear Parents,

We have been studying friendship in our classroom. We will be making a Friendship Salad as a class on _____.
                                                    date and time
Each student in our class will bring one ingredient to add to the salad. Please see the assignment for your child below:

- ❑ 2 apples
- ❑ 2 bananas
- ❑ 2 cans pineapple chunks
- ❑ 1 cup watermelon, seeded and cut into small pieces
- ❑ 1 cup cantaloupe, seeded and cut into small pieces
- ❑ 1 cup miniature marshmallows
- ❑ one 8-oz. carton of whipped topping
- ❑ one 8-oz. carton of fruit yogurt

If you have any questions, please do not hesitate to contact me.

Sincerely,

Friendship Traits

Match the sentences about friends with the correct pictures.

1. Katie and Cathy are swimming together.

2. Jeff and Jenna are playing marbles.

3. Elise is helping Anne learn to read.

4. Mike and Sarah share a Popsicle.

5. Samuel and John give each other a hug.

Letter to a Friend

Dear _____,

_____

_____

_____

_____

_____

_____

_____

_____

_____

_____

_____

_____

Sincerely,

Friendship Awards

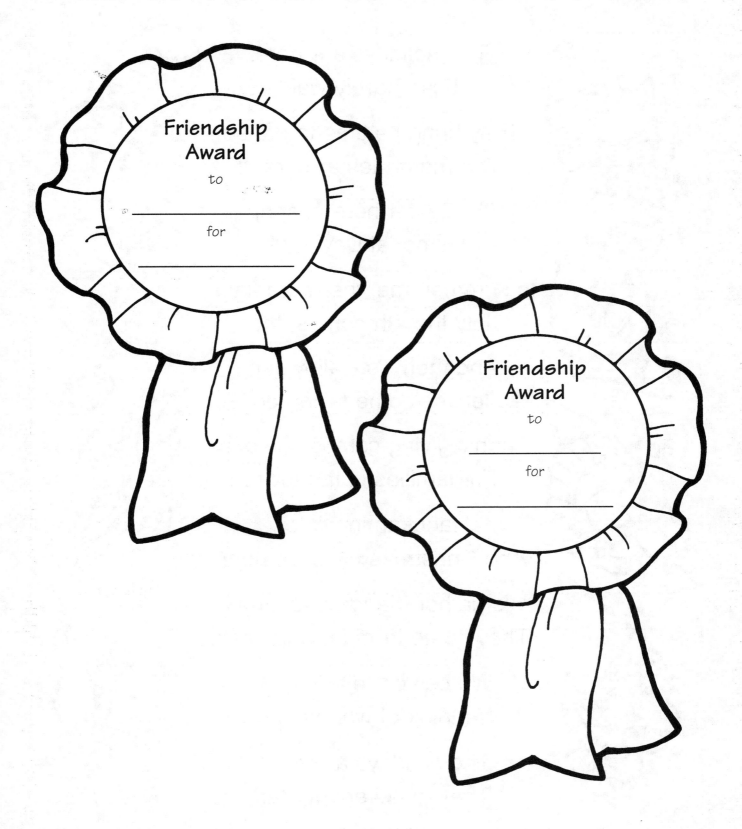

Happy Holidays

The holidays are here,
I can hardly wait!

They bring us time to pause;
The memories are great!

With Easter here in spring,
Memorial Day, too!

In summertime, there are flags,
July the 4th comes, too!

And then it's Halloween,
As leaves come falling down.

Thanksgiving comes so soon,
For families in the town.

Hanukah in winter,
And Christmas bells we hear.

We gather friends and family;
They come from far and near.

We celebrate our lives,
We think of who we are.

The holidays are here,
They're never very far!

Happy Holidays Lesson Plans

Week One

1. Begin the unit by asking students to tell you their favorite holiday. What do they like about this holiday? Explain that you are going to read a poem about holidays. Before reading, have the students list as many holidays as they can as you write them on the chalkboard.

2. Prior to the lesson, copy the poem on page 36 on chart paper. Read the poem aloud to the students. Encourage them to join in. After finishing the poem, ask students to help you read the poem again.

3. Distribute copies of the little book "Happy Holidays." Have students color the pages of their books and then cut them out. Help students assemble and staple their books together. Pair students with partners and have them read their little books together.

4. The focus for this little book is to identify and locate the holidays on a calendar. Holding a calendar, ask students to identify the holidays that occur during each month. Explain to the students that we celebrate holidays for different reasons.

5. Make a yearly calendar on your wall by posting a calendar for each month of the year. Use the blank calendar form on page 42 to decorate and fill in the numbers that correspond with each of the months. Spend this week learning about the holidays in the spring. These would be the holidays from March through May. Major American holidays during these months include St. Patrick's Day, Easter, May Day, and Memorial Day. Briefly discuss these holidays and their purpose. Invite students to share what they do with their families on these special days.

Week Two

1. Read "Happy Holidays" aloud to the students. Have them follow along in their little books. Point to each word as you read it. After reading the poem, have students look for words. Write the word *holidays* on the chalkboard and ask students to find and point to the word. Other words to look for include *spring, summer, fall, winter, Halloween, Thanksgiving, celebrate, families, friends,* and *life.*

2. Spend this week learning about the holidays in the summer, such as Flag Day and Fourth of July. Briefly discuss these holidays and why they are celebrated. Invite students to share what they do with their families on these special days.

3. Read "Happy Holidays" to the students. Prior to the reading, designate certain students to read different pages in the book. As you read the story, let students read their assigned pages. After reading the story, read other stories about the holidays. Encourage students to share what they have learned about the holidays from reading these books. (See the bibliography on page 96.)

Happy Holidays Lesson Plans *(cont.)*

Week Three

1. Make holiday shapes out of felt material. Using a flannelboard, have students use the felt pieces to act out the poem about the holidays. Give each student a felt holiday symbol to hold. Read "Happy Holidays" and have the students place their holiday symbols on the flannel board at the appropriate times.

2. Read the story again with the students while they follow along in their little books. Point to each word as you read it, but allow students to do more and more of the reading on their own.

3. Spend this week learning about the holidays in the fall, such as Halloween, Veteran's Day, and Thanksgiving Day. Briefly discuss these holidays. Invite students to share what they do with their families on these special days.

4. Supply each student with two fact cards from page 43. Have each student draw a picture and write about the holiday featured on each card. Post the holiday facts along with the illustrations.

Week Four

1. Explain that holidays take place throughout the world. Invite special guests to visit your classroom to talk about these holidays. These people can share how the same holidays are celebrated in different places or they can share about holidays that are celebrated in other parts of the world, but not in the United States.

2. Spend this week learning about the holidays in the winter, such as Hanukah, Kwanzaa, Christmas, New Year's Eve, and Valentine's Day. Briefly discuss these holidays. Invite students to share what they do with their families on these special days.

3. Help students make a seasons mobile. Distribute copies of page 44 of the seasons page. In each of the four boxes, have each student draw a picture of a holiday celebrated in each of the four seasons. Pictures should be of things each student does to celebrate seasons as a family. When completed, assist students in cutting the four season/holiday pictures into four boxes. Follow the directions on page 45 to help students design a holiday mobile.

4. Cut strips of paper and label each with the name of a holiday. Place the strips in a bowl. Have each student take a turn to select a strip of paper out of the bowl. That student then acts out something that is done during the holiday. For example, if a student selects Halloween, he or she might pretend to go trick-or-treating. The class members try to guess what holiday the student is dramatizing.

Social Studies Literacy in the Works

This page provides learning center suggestions that can be used to reinforce skills taught and discussed in the classroom. Select the centers that you think would best meet the needs of your students.

Math Center

- Make a copy of the calendar form on page 42 for each student. Each student selects a month for which to make a calendar. Have students write in the dates and days of the week. The student should then add any holidays that take place during that month and then decorate the calendar with symbols and pictures reflective of that month.

- Provide old calendars for students to look through. Have questions available for students to answer using these calendars. How many months are in a year? How many days are in a month? How many holidays are listed on these calendars? How many holidays are there in the summer, winter, spring, and fall? What other information do calendars give us?

Reading Center

- Set up an area in your room (complete with large beanbags, pillows, and chairs) for independent reading. Keep a shelf of books available at all times for students to read and browse. For this center, have different stories about the holidays. (See the bibliography on page 96.)

Art Center

- Select an easy holiday craft that your students can make at this center. Each day have a different holiday craft to make. Holiday craft suggestions include making an American flag out of construction paper, a paper plate spider, a snowman out of cotton balls, a Christmas tree made of craft sticks, valentines made of doilies, and orange construction paper pumpkins with decorated faces.

Writing Center

- Have each student write a story about a favorite holiday memory. What happened on that special day? What else can be shared about this memory? Have the student illustrate a picture to go with the memory.

- Create word rings by cutting out strips of paper. Punch a hole in each strip. Have each student write down a word from the holiday poem on each strip. Place the strips on a metal ring. After the words have been written and added to the ring, students can practice reading the words.

Dramatic Play Center

- Provide costumes and props that are appropriate for each of the holidays. Encourage students to work together to create and act out a holiday play. Set aside a time for students to perform their plays.

Making the Little Book

Happy Holidays

1

The holidays are here I can hardly wait!   2

They bring us time to pause; the memories are great!   3

With Easter here in Spring, Memorial Day, too! In summertime, there are flags. July the 4th comes, too!   4

40

Making the Little Book (cont.)

And then it's Halloween, as leaves come falling down. Thanksgiving comes so soon, for families in the town. 5

Hanukah in winter, and Christmas bells we hear. 6

We gather friends and family, they come from far and near. 7

We celebrate our lives, we think of who we are. The holidays are here, they're never very far! 8

The Calendar

Sunday	Monday	Tuesday	Wednesday	Thursday	Friday	Saturday

Holiday Fact Cards

Write what you know about the holiday. Draw a picture to go with it.

Holiday: _____

Write three things about this holiday:

_____

_____

_____

Draw a picture about this holiday:

Holiday: _____

Write three things about this holiday:

_____

_____

_____

Draw a picture about this holiday:

My Favorite Holiday

Spring	Summer
Fall	**Winter**

Holiday Mobile

A mobile is a hanging sculpture with moving parts. Use the directions below to make a hanging mobile with your students.

Materials

- copy of page 44 for each student
- crayons or colored markers
- plastic hanger for each student
- 4 lengths of yarn or thick string (approximately 12 inches [30 cm] long) for each student
- hole puncher
- scissors

Directions

1. Have each student illustrate pictures of holidays for each of the four seasons.

2. Have each student cut out their four season pictures.

3. Assist the student in punching a hole at the top of each of the four pictures.

4. Help the student tie each string to the hanger and then to one of the sheets of paper. Space the hanging pictures on the hanger.

Spring

Summer

Fall

Winter

People in Our Community

A doctor helps us when we are sick.

A police officer helps us stay safe.

A nurse helps us stay healthy.

A firefighter helps fight fires.

A sanitation worker helps keep
our town clean.

A postal worker delivers our mail.

A teacher helps us learn.

Thanks, everyone!

People in Our Community Lesson Plans

Week One

1. Ask students to tell who comes to help if a house catches on fire. Who will help you learn to read? Who delivers letters to you? Who takes our trash away? Who do we see when we are sick? Ask a question about each person mentioned in the story on page 46.

2. Read "People in Our Community." After you have read the poem, encourage the students to read it with you. Point to each word as you read it.

3. Discuss the people in this poem. Select a student to represent each of the people mentioned. Have the students perform actions that these people do in the community. Read the poem again. As each person is mentioned, the student dramatizes the action.

4. Discuss the meaning of the word *community* with your students. The focus of this little book is to describe jobs that people do in our community. If available, get pictures of each of the people mentioned in this story. Hold up each picture and discuss with students how important the jobs are that these people do. What would it be like if these people didn't help in our community? Ask students what they would like to do in the community when they grow up. Make a copy of page 52 and have each student draw a picture of himself or herself in a future job and complete the sentence on the page.

Week Two

1. Distribute copies of the little books. Have students color the pages of their books and then cut them out. Help students assemble and staple their books together. Pair students with partners and have them read their little books together.

2. Read "People in Our Community" aloud to students. Have students follow along in their little books. Point to each word as you read it. After reading the story, have students look for words. Write the word *helps* on the chalkboard and ask students to find and point to the word. Other words to look for are *doctor*, *nurse*, *postal worker*, *police officer*, *fire fighter*, and *sanitation worker*. Have students complete page 53.

3. Read the story again with your class. Encourage your class to follow along. Read the story using a high voice. Now try reading the story using a low voice, then a silly voice, a shy voice, etc. Vary this activity by creating a rhythm by tapping or clapping as you read the little book. First, clap with your hands, tap your head, tap your belly, and then tap your arm, your leg, your elbow, etc. Emphasize the rhythm and keep repeating it so that it is easy for your students to follow along.

People in Our Community Lesson Plans (cont.)

Week Three

1. Read "People in Our Community" with the students. Read the poem as a group. Next time, read it with one student reading aloud on each page while the other students listen and follow along.

2. Write the lines from the "People in Our Community" poem on sentence strips. Post the sentence strips out of order on the chalkboard tray. Have students assist you in placing the strips in order. Read the sentences again to check the sequence. Have students make changes as needed. Try reading the story with the sentence strips out of order. How can students tell where the strips go?

3. This week would be a good time to invite guest speakers to visit your classroom. Have a representative from each job that is mentioned in the story. Invite a doctor to visit to talk about what he or she does at his or her job. A nurse can come to speak about the responsibilities of his or her job. A police officer can discuss job and safety tips for students. A sanitation worker can share about what happens to trash.

Week Four

1. Read other stories with your class about people in the community. Refer to the bibliography on page 96 for suggestions.

2. Read the "People in Our Community" story again. Have a relay. Divide the students into groups of seven and have them line up. Give each student in the line a different person from the story to act out. For example, the first person in each line will imitate a doctor. When the first person finishes acting, the second person in each line acts like a police officer. The third imitates a nurse, the fourth is a firefighter, the fifth is a sanitation worker, the sixth is a postal worker, and the seventh is a teacher. Discuss the actions of each person ahead of time so that each person on the team knows what to do.

3. Understanding the jobs of the people in the community is very important. Read the descriptions of the community workers on page 54. Have students solve these problems together.

4. Use the directions on page 55 to make vests for the students in your class. Each student makes a vest to represent a different job in the community. Put on a play to bring the story of "People in Our Community" alive. Encourage students to determine what they will say for their parts. Set up a time to present this play to parents, another class, or to faithful workers in your community.

5. As your concluding activity for this unit, have students write letters of thanks to people from the community. Use the letter outline on page 34. Be sure to mail these letters.

Social Studies Literacy in the Works

This page provides learning center suggestions that can be used to reinforce skills taught and discussed in the classroom. Select the centers that you think would best meet the needs of your students.

Reading Center

• Set up an area in your room for independent reading. Provide beanbags, pillows, or chairs for more comfort. Keep a bookshelf of books available at all times for students to read and browse. For this center, provide stories about people in our community. (See the bibliography on page 96.)

• Write the lines of the poem on different sentence strips. At this center, have students work together to read the sentences and determine the correct sequence. Have a little book of this poem available for students to check their work.

Math Center

• Provide old newspapers for students to browse through. Have students locate examples of people in the community mentioned in the newspapers. Students are to cut them out and paste them onto a sheet of paper. The students then count the cut outs and write the number on the paper.

Writing Center

• Ask each student to write about an experience he or she has had with a member of the community. Have each student write about this experience in his or her literacy journal. (See page 5 for directions.) Have the student write as many words as possible about the experience. Then have the student illustrate the experience to provide more details.

Art Center

• Have students color pictures of community workers. When they have finished, cut the pictures into large puzzle pieces. Have students try to put their puzzles back together again. Store the puzzle pieces in envelopes for organization.

• Provide dough or clay for students to create scenes with community workers at work. Have students use blocks or other building materials to create their scenes.

Dramatic Play Center

• Have props and clothes available that represent the different jobs mentioned in the poem. Have students act out what the people in these different jobs do. Create a mini society in your classroom by setting up a post office, a police station, a fire station, a school, a doctor's office, and a recycling center. Have each student play the role of a community worker and interact with other students/community workers at this center.

People in Our Community

1

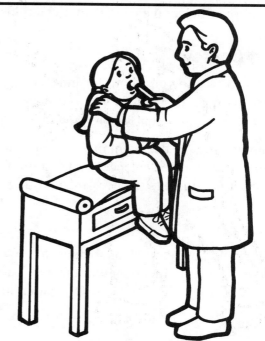

A doctor helps us when we are sick.   2

A police officer helps us stay safe.   3

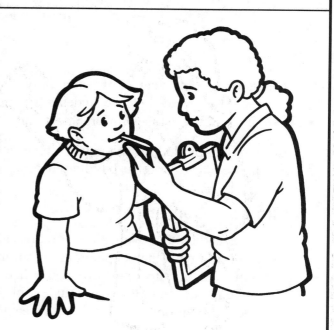

A nurse helps us stay healthy.   4

Making the Little Book *(cont.)*

A firefighter helps fight fires. 5

A sanitation worker helps keep our town clean. 6

A postal worker delivers our mail. 7

A teacher helps us learn. Thanks, everyone! 8

When I Grow Up...

When I grow up I want

to be _____

because _____

_____

_____.

Match the Job

Match the people with the tools they use.

Workers in Our Community

Read each of the descriptions below and ask your students to guess who is being described. Read one sentence at a time. Have students raise their hands when they think they know who is being described. When all the clues have been read, select a student to share the answer.

1. I drive a big truck. I like to keep things clean. I like to recycle. I take your trash away for you. I come on scheduled days. Who am I?

   Sanitation Worker

2. I can help keep you stay safe. I wear a uniform with a heavy helmet. I have important tools that I use. I need a long hose. The car or truck I drive has a siren on it because I am often in a hurry. I use water for my job. I put out fires as quickly as I can. Who am I?

   Fire Fighter

3. I usually wear scrubs. I like to help. I might work in a hospital, at a school, or in a doctor's office. I give shots, check your weight and height, and take your temperature. I help the doctor. Who am I?

   Nurse

4. I deal with stamps. I wear a uniform. I drive in a truck. I do my job in all kinds of weather. I work when it is sunny, rainy, or snowy. I take letters and envelopes in my truck. I deliver mail. Who am I?

   Postal Worker

5. I wear a uniform. I might drive a car or a motorcycle. My vehicle has a loud siren and lights on it. I need these things to get cars to stop. I might direct traffic or give out speeding tickets. I can even help a child find his or her way home. I help people stay safe and I try to catch people who break the law. Who am I?

   Police Officer

6. I usually wear a white lab coat. I work to make people feel better. People usually come see me when they are sick. I use a stethoscope to listen to your heart and lungs. I can give you medicine to make you feel better. I might work in a hospital or in a medical office. I work with nurses. Who am I?

   Doctor

7. I like kids. I help kids learn to read and do math. I work at a school. I work to educate people. I use books and other things to help people understand what I am teaching. I try to motivate all my students to do their best. Who am I?

   Teacher

Worker Vests

Help your students create uniforms for dressing up as community members. Each vest can be customized for the kind of community worker.

Materials

- brown paper grocery bag for each student
- poster paint
- paintbrush
- colored markers
- child safety scissors
- ribbon
- stapler

Directions

1. Lay the grocery bag flat with the opening at the bottom. Cut a vertical line from the opening of the bag to the opposite end.

2. Cut a round opening into what was the base of the bag. This will be the neck of the vest. Cut out arm holes on each side of the bag.

3. Cut two lengths of ribbon for laces to close the vest. Staple a strand of ribbon to either side of the vest opening.

4. Once the vests have been cut, have students try them on. Make adjustments as needed.

5. Using paint or the colored markers, have students decorate their vests.

6. When the vests are finished, have students try them on. Then, they can practice acting like the community worker.

My Senses

I have two eyes that let me see
The wondrous world in front of me!

And with my mouth, I get to eat,
And taste all things, both sour and sweet!

To help me smell, I have a nose.
I sniff fresh bread, I smell a rose.

I have two hands with which to touch
A kitten's fur, the grass, and such!

And with my ears, I get to hear
The sounds of things both far and near.

I'm glad they're here, my senses, five.
They help me learn and feel alive!

My Senses Lesson Plans

Week One

1. Ask students to tell you about the parts of their bodies. Ask students to point out their ears, noses, eyes, hands, feet, elbows, mouths, legs, arms, heads, and tummies. Tell students that you have a poem about five body parts. These are important body parts because they help us see, hear, smell, taste, and touch. Read the poem "My Senses." You may copy and enlarge page 56 to use for this activity. As you read the poem aloud, add expression and point to the body parts being described.

2. Read the poem again. When finished, ask students to list the body parts mentioned. Write each of these on the chalkboard. What sense goes with each of these five body parts? Have students share experiences they have had with each of these senses. What are their favorite sights? Smells? Sounds? Things to taste? Things to touch?

3. Point out to the students that there are rhyming words in this poem. Give them examples of rhyming words. Then ask students to locate the rhyming words—*see/me*, *eat/sweet*, *nose/rose*, *touch/such*, *hear/near*, *five/alive*. Using a highlighter marker, underline these rhyming words. Then read the poem again. As you read the poem this time, point to the rhyming word, but do not say it. Let the students read the word aloud.

4. The focus of this unit is identifying the five senses. Set up activities featuring the five senses in learning centers for your students to explore. (There are center suggestions on page 59.) After the center time, discuss the senses with your students and ask them what they learned.

5. Take your students on a walk outside. Encourage them to use the senses to explore the world. What do they see? What do they hear? What do they smell? How do things feel? Take a minute to focus on each sense so that it is easier to concentrate on just one at a time. For example, have students sit together somewhere outside. Ask the students to sit quietly for five minutes and listen. When the time is up, ask them to tell you what they heard. Focus on smells next, then sights, and then touch. Touching can include instructing your students to find something smooth, something pointed, something rough, something wet, something dry, etc. Use page 62 to record findings.

Week Two

1. Spend time discussing the ears. If possible, have a diagram, or a picture of an ear to show students how sound travels through it. Have students complete page 63.

2. Distribute copies of the little books. Have students color the pages and then cut them out. Help students assemble and staple their books together. Pair students with partners and have them read their little books together.

3. Read "My Senses" aloud. Have students follow along in their little books. Point to each word as you read it. Have students look for words. Write the word *senses* on the chalkboard. Ask students to point to the word in their books. Other words to look for are *see*, *smell*, *hear*, *touch*, *feel*, *eyes*, *ears*, *nose*, and *mouth*.

My Senses Lesson Plans *(cont.)*

Week Three

1. Have students retell the poem to check comprehension. What do each of the senses do? Make up silly sentences about each sense that is incorrect and ask the students to correct you. For example, "My mouth helps me to hear my favorite movie." Write the lines of the poem on different sentence strips. Post the sentence strips out of order on the chalkboard. Have students assist you in placing them in order. Read the sentences again to check the sequence. Make changes as needed.

2. Read "My Senses" to the students. Then read other books about senses and using our bodies to explore the world around us. (See the bibliography on page 96.) Discuss the similarities and differences between each story.

3. Read the story again with the students while they follow along in their little books. Point to each word as you read it, but allow students to do more and more of the reading on their own.

4. Discuss the sense of smell with students. If possible, show a picture of a nose. Distribute copies of page 64 for students to complete.

Week Four

1. Invite a student to draw a picture on the chalkboard of something he or she loves to eat. Have the other students guess what is being drawn. Then let another student draw a picture. Discuss the mouth with your students. You may wish to discuss taste buds and where they are located.

2. Show a picture of an eye. Have students draw or paint a pictures of things they love to look at. Post these eye-pleasing pictures in your classroom.

3. Set aside a day for your students to experiment with textures. Have students look at their hands. Blindfold a student volunteer. Then place an object in his or her hands. The student can use his or her hands to determine the identity of the object. The class members can not give clues. Let the student make a guess and then remove the blindfold. Now have another student come to the front. Be sure to have a variety of textures available for students to feel. Distribute copies of page 65 for students to complete.

4. Have your students conduct a science experiment at home. With the help of an adult, the student selects small pieces of food. The student blindfolds a family member and then gently places a clothespin on this person's nose. The student then gives a bite of food to the blindfolded family member to eat and determine what the food is without the use of smelling or seeing the object. Upon returning to school, have students discuss how seeing and smelling help us with the sense of taste. How else do the senses work together? Can you find your way across the room without your sense of sight? Encourage students to try other experiments and report their findings to the class.

Science Literacy in the Works

This page provides learning center suggestions that can be used to reinforce skills taught and discussed in the classroom. Select the centers that you think would best meet the needs of your students.

Science Center

- Provide slices of red and green apples at this center. Have students taste each type of apple and discuss the differences in the taste. Have students sample other differences between foods such as cereals, cheeses, and other fruit. Note: check for food allergies.

- Have students blow "smelly" bubbles. Add peppermint extract to soapy water. The smell will add another dimension to bubble blowing.

- Fill empty film canisters with different small objects, such as rice, nuts and bolts, beans, or paperclips. Mark the film canisters on the bottom with numbers. Have students shake the canisters and guess what is inside. Supply an answer key so students can check to see if their guesses were correct.

- Have students play "What's that sound?" Students turn their backs as another student makes a noise with an object. Students try to guess the object that made the sound.

Reading Center

- Write the lines of the poem on different sentence strips. At this center, have students work together to read the sentences and determine the correct sequence. Have a little book of this story available for students to check their work.

- Set up an area in your room for independent reading. Provide beanbags, pillows, or chairs for more comfort. For this center, have different books about the five senses available for students. (See Bibliography on page 96.)

Writing Center

- Have students write in their literacy journals (see page 5 for instructions) about experiences they have had using their senses. What things do they like about their senses? What would life be like without the ability to smell, touch, hear, see, or taste?

Art Center

- Set up an easel with paper. Have students paint patterns with watercolors. Encourage students to use as many different colors as possible to create striking visual images. Try this center again on a different day and have students paint blindfolded.

Making the Little Book

My Senses

1

I have two eyes that let me see the wondrous world in front of me!

2

And with my mouth, I get to eat, and taste all things, both sour and sweet!

3

To help me smell, I have a nose. I sniff fresh bread, I smell a rose.

4

Making the Little Book *(cont.)*

I have two hands with which to touch 5

A kitten's fur, the grass, and such! 6

And with my ears, I get to hear, the sounds of things, both far and near. 7

I'm glad they're here, my senses, five. They help me learn and feel alive! 8

My Senses Scavenger Hunt

Complete this page during your scavenger hunt. Draw pictures of the things you find.

Things I saw with my eyes:

Things I heard with my ears:

Things I smelled with my nose:

Things an animal could taste with its mouth:

Things I felt with my hands:

Things I Can Hear

Draw a line from the ear to the pictures of things that can be heard.

I Smell Something!

Draw circles around the five pictures of things that you can smell.

Touch and Texture

Write or draw pictures in each box.

Things that are smooth:	Things that are rough:
Things that are squishy:	**Things that are pointed:**

My Rock Book

Rocks are everywhere I go—

They're always close to me.

Rocks are in a mountain brook,

And rocks are in the sea.

Rocks along a country road,

And in the desert sand.

Rocks are found in city streets,

And all across the land.

My Rock Book Lesson Plans

Week One

1. Display a rock collection to share with your students. Discuss the differences between all of the rocks. Read "My Rock Book" to your class. Discuss this poem with the students. Ask them to suggest places where they see rocks. What do they do with rocks?

2. Read the story *Everybody Needs a Rock* by Byrd Baylor. (See the bibliography on page 96.) This is a story about how to select the perfect rock. If possible, go on a walk with your students to select the perfect rock. If you are not able to do this, invite each student to bring a rock from home. Remind them to choose rocks that are easy to handle and carry.

3. Have each student create a pet rock with the rock brought from home or found at school. Give the children an assortment of art materials to use, such as yarn, fabric trim, lace, wiggle eyes, scraps of fabric, construction paper, markers, and craft glue. Each rock can be transformed into a person, an animal, or an imaginary character.

4. Write lines of the poem on different sentence strips and have students use a pocket chart to practice sequencing skills. Have the students place the sentence strips in order. Next, mix up the strips and hand them to students. Invite them to put their sentence strip in the correct sequence without talking to any other class members. Place the strips and the pocket chart at your reading center for independent reading practice.

5. Make a copy of page 72 for students. Teach this song to your students. Have students perform the song for another class or for parents.

Week Two

1. The focus for this little book is to identify basic earth materials. Ask students to tell what they know about rocks. Record their answers on a three-column chart below the label *What I Know*. Then ask students what they want to know about rocks. Record these under the *Want to Know* heading. As you continue through this unit, periodically ask students to share what they have learned about rocks. Record these findings under a column labeled *Learned*.

2. Rocks come in all different sizes and shapes. Make copies of page 73 for students. This page has a rock activity that will help students determine the length of different rocks.

3. Read "My Rock Book" aloud. Have students follow along in their little books. Model how to point to each word as it is read. After reading the story, have students look for words. Write the word *rocks* on the chalkboard and ask students to find and point to the word. Other words to look for include *mountain*, *country road*, *desert*, *sea*, *city streets*, and *land*.

My Rock Lesson Plans *(cont.)*

Week Three

1. Read other stories about rocks with your students. (See the bibliography on page 96.) Discuss the similarities and differences between each story. Make a chart to compare the stories. What was the location of the rocks in the books? Across the top of the chart, have columns with headings, such as *mountain brook*, *sea*, *country road*, *desert*, *city streets*. Put a tally under each column for each of these places mentioned in the books.

2. Read the poem again with the students while they follow along in their little books. Point to each word as you read it, but allow students to do more and more of the reading on their own.

3. Go on a scavenger hunt on the grounds of your school. Have students be on the lookout for rocks being used. Rocks are used in buildings, walls, bridges, walkways, jewelry, or gravel. Make a list of the different uses for rocks.

4. Teach children to play games in which rocks are used. Use the game suggestions on page 74.

5. Help students create their own rock collections. Give each student an egg carton and write his or her name on it. Have students select rocks to add to their collections. Encourage them to find rocks with different shapes, sizes, colors, and textures. Be sure to set aside a time for students to share their rock collections with one another.

Week Four

1. Provide several nonfiction books about rocks and minerals. Allow time for students to browse through the books and gather as many facts and information they can. Have students share their findings in oral reports, paintings, or murals.

2. Have your students cut out pictures that begin with *r* for *rock* from magazines. Instruct the students to glue the pictures onto rock-shaped paper and display them in the reading center. Have children use pebbles to form letters or even spell words.

3. Make a copy of page 75 for each student. Provide a container of small pebbles and rocks. Challenge each youngster to guess the number of rocks he or she thinks can be picked up in one hand. The student writes the guess on the left hand. Then the student grabs a handful of rocks and counts them. On the right hand, the student records the actual number of rocks. The rocks are then glued down as evidence.

Science Literacy in the Works

This page provides learning center suggestions that can be used to reinforce skills taught and discussed in the classroom. Select the centers that you think would best meet the needs of your students.

Reading Center

- Provide sentence strips containing the lines from the poem. At this center, have students work together to read the sentences and determine the correct sequence. Have a little book of this story available for students to check their work.

- Have all the versions of stories and poems about rocks and minerals for students to browse on their own. Provide chairs, beanbags, or pillows to make it more comfortable. Also, display a poster of "My Rock Book" for students to point to and read.

Science Center

- Bring in a collection of different types of rocks. At this center, students can use magnifying glasses to explore the rocks and examine them close up. Have students categorize the rocks, based on color, texture, size, or other categories determined by the students.

Math Center

- Make a guessing jar by filling a large jar or container with rocks. You can have rocks of all different sizes or all similar sizes. Provide students with slips of paper to write their guesses of the number of rocks. When all students have determined their guesses, have students work together to count the rocks.

- Have a variety of rocks available for students to measure and weigh. Which rock weighs the most? Which rock weighs the least? Can you tell by looking? You can also have water in containers to determine whether the rocks will sink or float.

Art Center

- Set up an easel with paper. Have students use watercolor paints to paint pictures of the rocks in their natural environment. Have students draw rocks in the desert, in the mountains, in the ocean, on city streets, or in streams.

Writing Center

- Make mini-books for students to write their own stories about make-believe adventures with their pet rocks. Have students draw day-by-day pictures of what they do with their pet rocks.

Making the Little Book

My Rock Book

1

Rocks are everywhere I go— they're always close to me.

2

Rocks are in a mountain brook, 3

and rocks are in the sea. 4

Making the Little Book (cont.)

Rocks along a country road, 5

and in the desert sand. 6

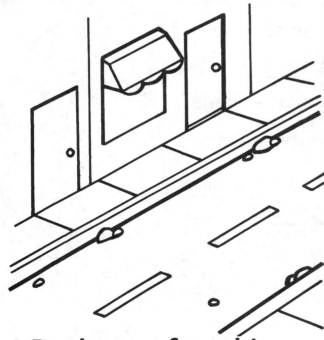

Rocks are found in city streets, 7

and all across the land. 8

The Rock Hound Song

(sung to the tune of "Mary Had a Little Lamb")

Here's a rock that I just found,

I just found,

I just found.

Here's a rock that I just found,

And now I have a friend.

My rock is gray and has a spot,

Has a spot,

Has a spot.

My rock is gray and has a spot,

It's also very smooth.

My rock's not big nor is it small,

Nor is it small,

Nor is it small.

My rock's not big nor is it small,

It's just the perfect size.

My rock is flat on just one side,

Just one side,

Just one side.

My rock is flat on just one side,

And bumpy on the other!

Note: The words of this song can be varied to match the characteristics of the rocks the children found.

Rock Search

Cut out the rock ruler at the bottom of the page and use it to measure rocks.

Can you find a rock that is about 1 inch (2.5 cm) long? Trace the rock here.

Can you find a rock that is less than 1 inch (2.5 cm) long? Trace the rock here.

Can you find a rock that is longer than 1 inch (2.5 cm)? Trace the rock here.

Select a rock of your choice. Measure how long your rock is. Write the answer in the box and then trace your rock here.

My Rock Ruler

Rock Games

There are many games and activities you can do with rocks. Here are some suggestions.

Guessing Game

Have a child place a rock in one hand. The child displays both clenched hands and classmates try to guess which hand is hiding the rock.

Hopscotch

Use sidewalk chalk to create the hopscotch grid. Write numbers in each of the spaces of the grid. Use rocks as markers for playing hopscotch. A child tosses a rock to a space in the hopscotch grid. Then the child hops on one foot through the hopscotch grid. When the child comes to the space with the rock, he or she must bend down and pick it up without losing balance, then continue hopping to the end of the grid.

Rock, Rock, Who has Your Rock?

Choose a child to sit in a chair placed in the center of a circle. Have this child close his or her eyes. Place a rock under the chair and select another student to sneak up and get the rock. This student returns to his or her place and puts the rock behind his or her back. Have all the students sit with their hands in their laps. The child sitting in the chair must guess who took the rock.

Crystal Garden

Make a crystal garden by taking a piece of charcoal and placing it in a disposable plastic bowl. Mix a solution of ½ cup (125 mL) liquid bluing, ½ cup (125 mL) water, and 1 cup (250 mL) ammonia. Pour it over the charcoal. (Add a few drops of food coloring too.) Watch the crystals grow over several days. Have students record their observations on a daily basis.

Create a Fossil

Each student will need:

- 1 ½ pint (700 mL) milk carton cleaned and dried. (Cut off the top section.)
- 1 bar of modeling clay
- choice of fossil items such as shells, leaves, bones, etc.

Have the students press their clay into the bottom of their cartons and smooth out the top of the clay. Press the fossil item firmly into the clay and remove. Prepare a mixture of plaster of Paris and pour a layer over each impression until it is covered. Set aside to dry. Tear the carton away from the clay and plaster to reveal a "fossil."

Estimating Rocks

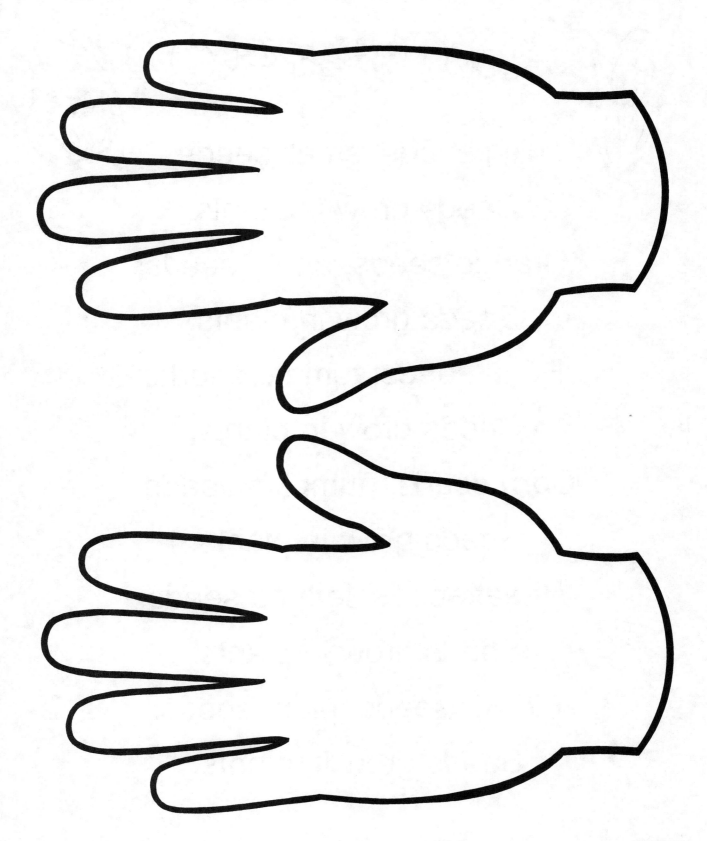

Watch it Grow!

Big seeds, small seeds;

Seeds grow in plants.

Orange seeds, apple seeds;

Seeds grow in plants.

Bean seeds, tomato seeds;

Seeds grow in plants.

Corn seeds, pumpkin seeds;

Seeds grow in plants.

Wheat seeds, lettuce seeds;

Seeds grow in plants.

Flower seeds, plant seeds;

Seeds grow in plants.

Watch It Grow! Lesson Plans

Week One

1. Ask students if they have ever seen a seed. Have samples of different types of seeds available for students to look at. Have them guess what type of plant is grown from each seed. Be sure to have a variety of sizes and colors of seeds. Discuss with students how they think the seeds grow. Discuss the three main ingredients that all seeds need in order to grow. These things are soil, water, and sunlight. All seeds need different amounts of these things. Read the poem "Watch it Grow!" You may copy and enlarge page 76 to use for this activity.

2. Ask students to tell you the different foods/plants that were mentioned in the poem. Have samples of these foods/plants available for students to look at. Ask students to find seeds in these plants. If possible, have plants at different stages available for students to observe. Show them the seed, the seedling, the small plant, and the large plant. Remind them that soil, water, and sunlight are needed to grow these seedlings. Reproduce and cut out the cards on page 82. Have students put them in the right order.

3. Read the poem again. Prior to reading the poem, use a cloze technique by covering words and asking students to name the missing word. Move the pieces of paper and cover up different words to determine whether the students can fill in the covered word. If time allows, have students use adhesive notes to cover up words in the poem for other students to fill in.

Week Two

1. Discuss with students the different stages of the plant. Write each of these on the chalkboard. (These are seed, seedling, small plant, large plant.) Under each heading, have students share characteristics and comparisons. Write these on the chalkboard.

2. The focus of this little book is to perform simple comparisons and experiments. Explain to students that they will be growing seeds and plants of their own. First, you will try an experiment with seeds and plants. With your students observing, plant four seeds in separate Styrofoam cups. Label each cup with a number 1, 2, 3, or 4. In cup number 1, plant the seed without soil, but water it daily and keep it in the window. In cup number two, plant the seed in soil, and place it in the window, but do not water it. In cup number 3, plant the seed and water it daily, but store it in a closet where it receives no sunlight. In cup number 4, plant the seed in soil, water it daily, and store it in the window where it will get plenty of sunlight. Each day compare the four plants. What is happening to the three cups that are missing one of the important ingredients? Discuss observations as a class.

3. Distribute copies of the little books "Watch it Grow!" Have students color the pages of this book and then cut them out. Help students assemble and staple their books together. Divide students into pairs and have them read their little books together. Use a variety of methods to read the little book with your students.

Watch it Grow! Lesson Plans (cont.)

Week Three

1. Read "Watch It Grow!" to students from a little book like theirs. Have them follow along in their little books. Write the word *seed* on the chalkboard and ask students to find and point to the word. Other words to look for are *orange, apple, bean, tomato, corn, pumpkin, wheat,* and *lettuce.* Now read a different story about seeds and plants. Discuss these books with your students. What have they learned about seeds and plants? (See the bibliography on page 96.)

2. Read the poem again with the students while they follow along in their little books. Point to each word as you read it, but this time, do not say all the words. Point to a word without reading it and have students read it. Allow students to do more of the reading.

3. Bring a flower to class to use in a discussion about plant parts. Help students locate the roots, the flower, the leaf, the seeds, and the stem of the flower. Have other plants available for students to locate these parts as well. When finished, distribute copies of page 83 and have students cut and paste the words to the correct plant parts.

4. Help your students perform a science experiment by planting a seed. Corn or grass seed grows quickly and are easy to plant. You will need a Styrofoam cup, two or three seeds, potting soil, water, and a place with plenty of sunshine. Show students how to push the seed into the soil so that it is just covered. Have students write a hypothesis as to when their seed plant will poke through the soil. Make copies of page 84 and have students make plant observation journals to document the growth of their plants each day. Each day students will write in their journals, and then draw sketches of the plants to document growth.

Week Four

1. Display a variety of nonfiction books available about seeds and plants. Allow time for students to browse through the books and gather information. Have students share their findings with the class. Make a list of facts that students have found about seeds and plants.

2. On the chalkboard, write "My seed will…." Then have students copy these words and add an ending to the sentence. Remind them to write a period at the end of the sentence. Provide crayons or colored pencils for illustrating their sentences. Have a sharing time for students to share their sentences. Bind all pages together to create a book. Make a cover for this book and store it in the class library. Be sure to read the story aloud with students.

3. Have your students brainstorm a list of foods that come from seeds. Discuss how many of the vitamins and nutrients our bodies need come from these plants. As a class, make a plant soup. Invite parents to donate vegetables to help make the soup. On cooking day, clean, chop, and mix all of the vegetables. Add water and spices and simmer the soup until the vegetables have softened. Serve warm.

4. Distribute copies of page 85 to the students. You will need packets of carrot seeds, watermelon seeds, pumpkin seeds, apple seeds, and tomato seeds. Do not let the students see the pictures on the seed packets. Instruct the students to draw pictures of the seeds that they think go with each plant. When all students have finished, show them the seed that goes with each plant.

Science Literacy in the Works

This page provides learning center suggestions that can be used to reinforce skills taught and discussed in the classroom. Select the centers that you think would best meet the needs of your students.

Science Center

- Have soil and seeds available for students to practice planting seeds. You might want to designate a place outside your classroom for a garden. Have students use craft sticks and construction paper to make signs telling what has been planted.

- Have a variety of plants or food that have been grown in a garden. See how many of these food items your students can identify, such as celery, eggplant, okra, watermelon, cantaloupe, apples, bananas, and bell peppers.

Reading Center

- Have sentence strips containing the lines from the "Watch It Grow!" poem. At this center, have students work together to read the sentences and figure out the sequence of the poem. Have a little book of this poem available for students to check their work.

- Display nonfiction books, magazine articles, and posters about seeds. Have students browse these materials to learn more about seeds. Arrange a time in the day to have students report to the class what they have learned about seeds.

- Set up an area in your room for independent reading. Provide beanbags, pillows, or chairs for more comfort. Keep a bookshelf of books available at all times for students to read and browse. These can be stories about gardens, foods that come from plants, and seeds.

Art Center

- Have students color pictures of things they wish to eat that come from a garden. What types of foods would they like to cook for dinner? Have paper plates available and have students color pictures of plants that can be served for dinner.

- Use a variety of fruits and vegetables, such as carrots, potatoes, and apples, to make prints. Put several colors of tempera paints in disposable metal pie tins. Children dip the fruits and vegetables into the paint and make prints on sheets of paper. Model this for students first. Have them add words to tell what plants made the prints.

Dramatic Play Center

- Have cooking utensils available along with pots and pans for students to "cook" a dinner of plants. Provide plastic vegetables and fruits for students to serve each other as healthy meals.

Writing Center

- Make mini-books for students to write their own stories about planting a garden. Have students cut out pictures of fruits and vegetables to help illustrate their stories. Be sure to remind them to create titles for their stories.

Making the Little Book

Watch It Grow!

1

Big seeds, small seeds;

Seeds grow in plants. 2

Orange seeds, apple seeds;

Seeds grow in plants. 3

Bean seeds, tomato seeds;

Seeds grow in plants. 4

80

Making the Little Book *(cont.)*

**Corn seeds,
pumpkin seeds;**

Seeds grow in plants. 5

**Wheat seeds,
lettuce seeds;**

Seeds grow in plants. 6

**Flower seeds,
plant seeds,**

Seeds grow in plants. 7

The End 8

Seed to Plant Sequencing

Cut the cards out. Place them in the correct order.

82

Parts of a Plant

Color the plant. Cut out the word labels on the dotted lines. Match the words to the corresponding plant parts. Glue the labels in the word boxes.

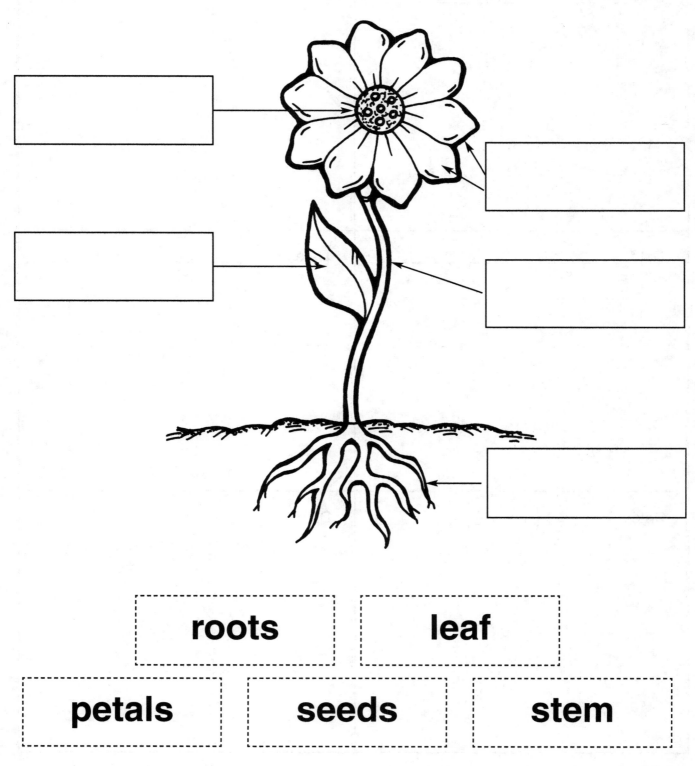

roots

leaf

petals

seeds

stem

Plant Observation Journal

Record the date. Draw a picture of what your seed or plant looks like each day. Cut the squares out and staple them together in order.

Date _____	Date _____
Date _____	Date _____
Date _____	Date _____

Seed Matching

Look at the pictures of the fruits and vegetables on the left. Can you match the seeds with the plants? Draw a picture of what you think the seed looks like. Check with your teacher to see if you are correct.

Fruits and Vegetables   **Draw the Seed**

My Book of Weather

What kind of weather
will be coming here today?
Should I stay indoors, or go outside to play?

If the weather's hot, I'll be playing in the sun.
My clothes will be just right; in shorts I will have fun.

And if it should be rainy, I'll keep from getting wet.
I'll open my umbrella and then I will be set.

But if it might be snowing, my hat will be on my head.
Gloves and boots will warm me when I get on my sled.

And if the weather's windy and freezes off my nose,
I'll be so very glad, I'll wear my warmest clothes.

And if it should be foggy, so I can hardly see.
Be careful and watch out, you might bump into me!

What kind of weather will be coming here today?
Should I stay indoors or go outside to play?

Weather Lesson Plans

Week One

1. Ask students to tell you about their favorite kind of weather. What day do they like the most? Do they like it when it is rainy, snowy, windy, or sunny? What makes it rain or snow or be windy outside? Explain that this is called the weather. What other facts do the students know about weather?

2. Read the poem "My Book of Weather" on page 86. Discuss the poem with students. You may use these questions:

   - Why do you need to wear different clothes based on what the weather is like?
   - Why don't we wear bathing suits every day?
   - What would happen if we wore coats every day?
   - When would be a good day to wear a hat?

3. Explain to students that the focus of this poem is to identify how weather affects daily activities. Show a globe to your students. Explain that this globe represents the world. Explain that there are different types of weather going on all over the world. If it is sunny where you are, there is rain and snow falling somewhere else. Have students brainstorm the different kinds weather. List these on the chalkboard. Take students outside to see what kind of weather is happening today.

4. Make a copy of page 92 and explain to students that you will keep track of the weather each day. Choose to do this as a class or make a copy for each child to record individually. Make weather predictions at the beginning of the day and see if the predictions end up being accurate at the end of the day. Extend this activity by recording the temperature each day. Point out the relationship between the rise and fall of the temperature and the kind of weather.

Week Two

1. Distribute copies of the little books "My Book of Weather" to the students. Have them color the pages and then cut them out. Help students assemble and staple their books together. Pair students with partners and have them read their little books together.

2. Read "My Book of Weather" aloud. Have students follow along in their little books. Point to each word as you read it. After reading the story, have students look for words. Write the word *weather* on the chalkboard and ask them to locate and point to it. Other words to look for are *hot*, *sun*, *rainy*, *wet*, *snowing*, *boots*, *sled*, *windy*, *warmest*, *foggy*, and *bump*. Add weather words to your word wall (see page 5).

4. Discuss the weather with your students. Distribute copies of page 93. Have students illustrate pictures of each kind of day listed on this page. What types of things would be in a rainy day picture that wouldn't be in a sunny day picture? What is the difference between a snowy day and a rainy day? Be sure that each student includes a person in the picture so he or she can show what kind of clothing needs to be worn on that day.

Weather Lesson Plans (cont.)

Week Three

1. Have students retell the poem about the weather to check comprehension. Make up statements about the poem that do not exist and have students correct you.

2. Invite a weather reporter or someone who has knowledge about weather to come and speak to your class. Perhaps the guest speaker could bring artifacts or pictures of weather storms and events from the past. What kinds of weather does the community in which you live experience? What are the hottest and lowest temperatures ever recorded?

3. Read "My Book of Weather" to the students. Now, have students close their little books. Write the lines of the poem on different sentence strips. Have your class work together to put these lines in order. Were the lines and words in correct order? Make changes as needed.

4. Read the story again with the students while they follow along in their little books. Point to each word as you read it, but allow students to do more and more of the reading on their own.

5. As an art activity, supply students with copies of page 94. This has a pattern to make a pinwheel. Once the pinwheel has been made, take the students outside to see if their pinwheels work. Explain to students that the pinwheel can be a weather tool to determine how windy it is outside.

Week Four

1. Read other stories about weather. A fun story to read is *Cloudy With a Chance of Meatballs* by Judi Barrett. Refer to the bibliography on page 96 for other suggestions.

2. Here is an experiment you can do to make it "rain" in your classroom. Fill a tea kettle about two-thirds full with water and place it on a hot plate. Hold a metal cake pan filled with ice cubes over the spout. As the water in the kettle boils and the steam begins to come out of the spout, condensation will form on the bottom of the pan. When enough condensation collects, it will "rain." Try to have a plant sitting next to the hot plate so the rain will fall on the plant. Discuss this experiment with your students.

3. Make copies of page 95 for students to make their own mini-books about seasons. Read these mini-books with students. When you have finished, divide your students into four groups. Give each group a large sheet of bulletin-board paper. Assign each group a season to illustrate. Display these murals in sequence.

Science Literacy in the Works

This page provides learning center suggestions that can be used to reinforce skills taught and discussed in the classroom. Select the centers that you think would best meet the needs of your students.

Science Center

- Show your students what a weather forecast in the newspaper looks like. Provide newspapers for students to look through to find weather forecasts to cut out.

- Have a globe available for your students to use in locating which parts of the earth are near the equator and have hot, steamy weather, and which parts are near the poles and have very cold weather.

Writing Center

- Have students write in their literacy journals (see page 5) about weather storms they have experienced. What was the scariest weather storm? What changed in the world as a result of this storm? Was there a flood? An earthquake? A tornado?

- Have students write stories about storms. Have students draw pictures to go with their stories. Create blank little books for students to use to write and illustrate their stories.

Reading Center

- Set up an area in your room for independent reading. Provide large beanbags, pillows, or chairs for more comfort. Keep a bookshelf of books about weather available for students to read and compare.

Listening Center

- Record a tape of different weather sounds and ask students to identify thunder, rain, snow, hail, wind, and other weather sounds. Extend this center by asking students to create their own storm sounds.

Art Center

- Have students paint bright yellow suns wearing sunglasses.

- Make paper kites with tails to display in your room.

- Do a crayon-resist snowy day picture by drawing a snowy scene on manila paper. Brush diluted blue paint over the picture for the crayon resist.

- Use gray construction paper background for a cloudy scene. Add white cotton balls for clouds, blue raindrops, and gold glitter for lightning.

Dramatic Play Center

- Provide several kinds of coats, scarves, gloves, mittens, hats, sunglasses, umbrellas, and other clothing and have students wear them as they act out different weather scenarios. Provide white packing peanuts to represent snow.

Making the Little Book

What kind of weather will be coming today?

1

If the weather's hot, I'll be playing in the sun.

2

And if it's rainy, I'll open my umbrella and I'll be set.

3

But if it might be snowing, Gloves and boots will keep me warm.

4

Making the Little Book (cont.)

And if the weather's windy, I'll be glad my hat is on my head! 5

And if it should be foggy, 6

Be careful and watch out, you might bump into me! 7

Should I stay indoors or go outside to play? 8

Weather Observation Chart

Weather Chart

						Fri.
						Thur.
						Wed.
						Tues.
						Mon.
						Fri.
						Thur.
						Wed.
						Tues.
						Mon.
sunny	windy	rainy	overcast	foggy	cold	

Weather Days

Draw a picture of what the day looks like when it is sunny, snowy, rainy, or windy outside.

Sunny Day	Snowy Day
Rainy Day	**Windy Day**

Making a Pinwheel

Cut along the dotted lines. Bring all the corners marked "A" together to meet in the center. Pin the four corners through the center of the square dot. Push the pin into a pencil eraser. Blow on the pinwheel to test it.

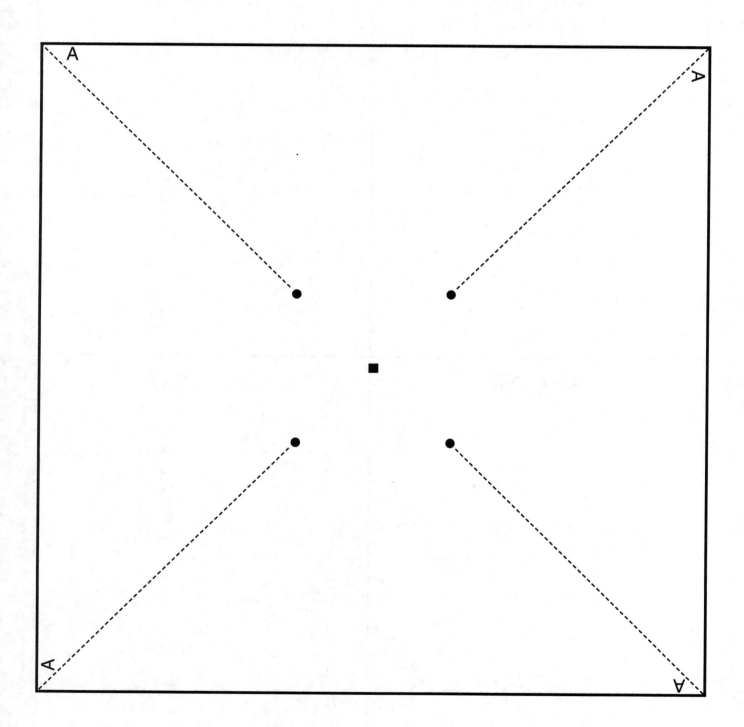

Mini-Book of Seasons

Color and cut out each box. Then staple the pages together.

My Mini-Book of
Seasons

by _____

1

It is winter.

2

It snows in the winter.

3

It is spring.

4

It rains in the spring.

5

It is summer.

6

It is hot in the summer.

7

It is fall.

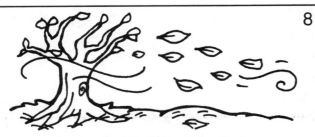

8

Leaves fall in the fall.

9

There are four seasons—winter, spring, summer, and fall.

Bibliography

Fiction

Ahlberg, Janet and Allen. *Starting School*. Viking Kestrel, 1998.

Aliki. *My Five Senses*. HarperCollins, 1989.

————. *We are Best Friends*. Mulberry Books, 1982.

Baer, Edith. *This is the Way We Go to School*. Scholastic, 1992.

Barrett, Judi. *Cloudy with a Chance of Meatballs*. Aladdin Library, 1982.

Berenstain, Stan and Jan. *The Berenstain Bears Go to School*. Random House, 1978.

Brown, Marcia. *Stone Soup*. Scribner, 1975.

Carlson, Nancy. *I Like Me!* Viking Penguin, 1988.

Cohen, Miriam. *Best Friends*. Macmillan, 1971.

————. *Will I have a Friend?* Macmillan, 1967.

Hennessey, B.G. *School Days*. Viking, 1990.

Henrietta. *A Mouse in the House*. Dorling Kindersley, 1991.

Lobel, Arnold. *Frog and Toad are Friends*. Harper and Row, Jr., 1979.

Mayer, Mercer. *All by Myself*. Western Publishing, Co. Inc., 1983.

McCully, Emily Arnold. *School*. Harper & Row, 1987.

Moulten, Mark Kimball. *A Snowman Named Just Bob*. Lang Books, 1999.

————. *Miss Fiona's Stupendous Pumpkin Pies*. Lang Books, 2001.

Munsch, Robert. *Love You Forever*. Firefly Books, Ltd., 1989.

Schweninger, Ann. *Off to School!* Viking Penguin, 1987.

Sharmat, Marjorie Weinman. *I'm Terrific*. Holiday House, Inc., 1988.

Showers, Paul. *The Listening Walk*. HarperCollins, 1991.

VanAllsburg, Chris. *The Polar Express*. Houghton Mifflin, 1985.

Nonfiction

Barkan, Joanne. *Rocks, Rocks, Big and Small*. Silver Press, 1990.

Baylor, Byrd. *Everybody Needs a Rock*. Scribner, 1974.

Cole, Joanna. *The Magic School Bus Inside the Earth*. Scholastic, 1987.

Fowler, Allan. *What's the Weather Today?* Children's Press, 1991.

————. *Seeing Things, Hearing Things, etc…*. Children's Press, 1991.

Gans, Roma. *Rock Collecting*. Harper & Row, 1984.

Gibbons, Gail. *From Seed to Plant*. Holiday House, 1991.

————. *Weather Words and What They Mean*. Holiday House, 1990.

Heller, Ruth. *The Season for a Flower*. Putnam, 1983.

Intrater, Roberta Grobel. *Two Eyes, a Nose and a Mouth*. Scholastic, 1995.

Jordan, Helene J. *How a Seed Grows*. HarperCollins, 1992.

Kotte, Jan. *A Day with a Mail Carrier*. Children's Press, 2000.

————. *A Day with a Police Officer*. Children's Press, 2000.

————. *A Day with Fire Fighters*. Children's Press, 2000.

Lottridge, Celia Baker. *One Watermelon Seed*. Oxford University Press, 1985.

Palazzo, Janet. *What Makes Weather?* Troll, 1982.